Ladies Keep it Movin'

Ladies Keep it Movin'

10 Steps for Staying Sane

and Fabulous

with Kids your Man

and a DREAM!

Christine FREE

Published by Belfrey Books

Copyright © 2011 by Christine Belfrey Johnson

all rights reserved,

No part of this publication may be reproduced, distributed, or transmitted in any form or by any means, without the prior written permission of the publisher, except in the case of brief quotations embodied in critical reviews and certain other noncommercial uses permitted by copyright law.

Second Belfrey Books Edition 2012

For information address:

BELFREY BOOKS

275 East 4th Street Suite 400
Saint Paul, MN. 55101

www.christinefree.com

Printed in the United States of America

Publisher's Cataloging-in-Publication data
FREE, Christine
Ladies Keep It Movin' : 10 Steps for Staying Sane & Fabulous with Kids, Your Man and a DREAM!
p. cm.

ISBN 978-0-9836504-3-0
1. Self Help – Personal Development 2. Mind, Body, Spirit - Religious Aspects 3. Parenting – Motherhood 4. Marriage

Acknowledgments

This book would not be possible without the strength and guidance of God. For this, I give thanks, for I know that all things are possible through him. He gives me continuous hope to dream on.

Thanks to my husband, Nathan for his patience and contributing efforts in making my dream a reality.

My children, Imani, Caleb, Ellis and Issa for being the biggest fans of my music, I love you deeply.

My mother Delores and father Wes for their love, support, guidance, wisdom and countless hours of baby sitting and prayers.

My sister Dionne and brother Christopher for their love and support.

My nieces and nephews that I love and for hours of baby sitting.

My brother in law and music producer Jacob, for being one of the first to take a chance and believe in me.

My cousin Tearza for giving me the idea for this book and believing in my dreams.

My Grandmothers, Louise and Christine for their strength, wisdom, gifts and bloodline.

My mother in law Carol for her pearls of wisdom and countless listening hours.

My aunts and uncles for pushing me to be my best.

My copy editor, Suze Allen graphic designer Jamacia Johnson and photographer Julian Murray for their contributing talents.

My Girlfriends, Angie, Nicole, Tinkle, Veda, Tameka, Alnita, Donecia, Stephanie, Ife, Margaux, Ashani, Tincy, Adrece, Chandra, Debbie, Sean, Miata, Ladiva, Fadina, Fatou, and Nita.

My church, Key Of Faith for allowing me to grow in every way as a woman.

This Book is dedicated with love to

My four beautiful Angels,
Imani, Caleb, Ellis and Issa
who have helped fuel my dreams.
A new dream was born with the birth of each child.

Table of Contents

Acknowledgments
5

Introduction
11

Section 1
How to Stay Sane Nurturing the Inner Me, Woman, Mother, Wife, and Lover
13

Step 1
Take Care of Yourself First Mind, Body, and Spirit
15

Step 2
Be True to Who You Are! Aside from Being a Mom and a Wife
29

Step 3
Dare to Dream! And Find Your Passion
35

Step 4
Slow Down, Breathe and Relax!
45

Section 2
How to Stay Sane Balancing Family, Kids, Husband, and Work
51

Step 5
Get Organized - Calendars and Routines Are a Necessity
53

Step 6
Don't Be Afraid to Ask or Pay for Help, You Can't Do It All! It Takes a Village
59

Step 7
Make Time for Family, Yeah!
65

Step 8
Realize They Ain't Perfect But They're Yours!
69

Section 3
Me My Fabulous Self and I
75

Step 9
How to be Fabulous (Or Fake It 'Til You Make It!)
77

Step 10
Don't Stay Stuck, How to Keep it Movin'
85

Appendix
93

Appendix A
Steps to Put Together Portfolio Christine's Plan
95

Appendix B
Song Lyrics by Christine Free
99

Appendix C
Sample Letters and Proposal Christine's Proposal
111

Introduction

Women frequently come up to me asking me how I do it. How, as a mother of four, am I able to find time for myself and still have the energy to pursue being an inspirational author, singer, and motivational speaker who will one day appear on the Oprah Winfrey Network? How do I push past all the busyness of my day and take the necessary steps to make my life what I want it to be? How do I juggle kids, husband, and a job while pursuing my dreams and taking care of myself? In the midst of it all, I have found several ways to help me persevere and have balance in my life. I will be the first to admit that the journey along the way has been challenging at times but a blessing, as long as I continue to persevere and keep it movin'. So for all the women who have asked, here's how I do it!

Section 1

How to Stay Sane Nurturing the Inner Me, Woman, Mother, Wife, and Lover

Step 1
Take Care of Yourself First Mind, Body, and Spirit

Put yourself first. Put yourself first. Put yourself first. I realize that may sound selfish, but the reality is that a lot of us do just the opposite and put ourselves last. And boy does it show in our health, our eyes, our spirit, our butt, our gut or our thighs!

In order to stay sane and healthy as a mother, lover or wife, there are times when putting yourself first is a must. Okay ladies, that doesn't mean going out and splurging on that Coach bag before buying groceries for the household (whoops, I may have done that!) or hanging all day with the ladies sipping Mai Tai's on the beach before taking care of your children and checking in with your man (what a nice fantasy, though).

The kind of putting yourself first that I'm talking about is realizing that as a nurturer if you aren't well - mentally, physically, and spiritually, you can't give what you don't have. And let me just say here that you don't have to be a mother in the sense of having birthed children. You might be acting as a mother figure to nieces, nephews, husbands, boyfriends or your community. Regardless of what kind of mother you are you still have to put yourself first to recharge.

Some of us have been brought up to believe that we can do it all even if we're deathly sick. There is a hidden expectation, to push ourselves beyond our limits and be Superwoman. After all, if we don't do everything in the house, who will? I know that there have been numerous times when I was sick and continued to work in the house and take care of everyone else without taking the time to just let go and take care of myself. As a result I often times felt burned out, depressed or numb to life.

I am reminded of the time when I got sick when I was 6 months pregnant with twins. I had been vomiting all night and went into the hospital the next morning to get some relief. I remember saying to the doctor, "Wow, this is great, I can finally rest and get pampered - in a sense." The doctor and nurse who were hooking up an IV of fluids in one arm (due to dehydration) and putting a needle in the other arm to draw my blood, told me I was a trooper.

"No, just a mom", I replied. They laughed and then we had a moment of silent understanding. They knew what I meant by that comment. That all mothers have to be strong, resilient, and push past our own needs to take care of others. And we know why we do it! Do you think that man of yours would be able to take care of the kids, the laundry, and hold life together if he were sick? Yeah, No! As soon as a man gets a sniffle it's over, he's shut down and demanding immediate attention. Please! Now don't get me wrong, my intentions are not to "male bash", as my husband would say, but to tell the simple truth - ladies if we don't take care of ourselves who will?

And care taking isn't just physical, right? When the twins were around 16 months, Caleb was 3 years old and Imani was 12, I went through several mentally and emotionally challenging periods. I was overwhelmed and anxious when dealing with my family. At times I didn't have enough patience stored up for my kids or husband and I was a bit on the edge. I felt stressed and sad. I was blessed to receive advice from someone who reminded me that I am human and what I was feeling was understandable and that it's okay to let off a little steam every now and then. I realized that I had been at a standstill with exercising, writing, and singing and I was losing a vital part of myself to the kids, my husband and the house. All the things that helped me to refuel and energize my body and spirit had taken a backseat and it began to show in my body, spirit and actions. I had to get it back. I needed to get back up and focus on my passions and dreams for my sake and the sake of my family.

If you've ever felt like that, go with me a little further here. In spite of the fact that mothers have a limited amount of time to read or focus on something other than the Disney channel, running errands, or cooking dinner (whew, sounds exhausting), it is possible for even the busiest of moms to take care of themselves. Here's how you can make it work.

A.) Your Mind - Nurture and Feed it!
Try, try, and try to take 10 to 20 minutes a day, typically in the morning before the rat race begins, or at night when the children are sound asleep (thank God!) to read something that will nourish your mind and soul that will allow time to unwind. Whether it's a positive quote dealing with appreciating life or opening you up to a new idea, reading a scripture from the bible that gives you a new perspective, or reading a chapter in a good book or an article in a magazine. Now, don't beat yourself up if you are unable to do this every day but make that the goal, because it will make a marked difference in how well you'll be able to handle the stressors of your day, allowing you to have down time.

Some of my favorite inspirational quotes and scriptures dealing with life and motherhood are the following:
- "A happy thought is like a seed that sows positivity for all to reap." Miriam Muhammad
- "What is success in this world? I would say it consist of four things. To live a lot, to love a lot, to laugh a lot, and from it all to learn a lot." Richard J. Needham
- "I can do all things through Christ who strengthens me." Philippians 4:13

- "Anything is possible. You can be told that you have a 90% chance or a 50% chance or a 1% chance, but you have to believe and you have to fight." Lance Armstrong
- "When you play, play hard; when you work, don't play at all." Theodore Roosevelt
- The Serenity prayer. "God grant me the Serenity to accept the things I cannot change, the Courage to change the things I can, and the Wisdom to know the difference." Reinhold Niebuhr
- "Cleaning your house while your kids are still growing is like shoveling snow while it's still snowing." Phyllis Diller, Comedian
- "Women complain about Premenstrual Syndrome, but I think of it as the only time of the month I can be myself." Roseanne Barr, Comedian

Make Space for Nourishing Your Mind and Soul. You may like to have an area or place in your house, that can serve as a sanctuary, like a corner of a desk, the basement or the walk-in closet where you can put up positive quotes or inspirational scriptures, and keep a candle and other important mementoes. A place where you can get away from the business of the day and dream. Where you can be alone and pray, think, reflect, give thanks, meditate, be inspired, appreciate, write and breathe. It's important to find a spot somewhere in your house where you can try, try, try to be alone and focus your mind.

B.) Your Body - Refresh it!
Ladies, we definitely could take better care of the body we have, right? You know the old saying, "you are what you eat" and boy, does it show. And having children is not a free pass to let go of ourselves in every way.

Believe me, I know it's a struggle to try to stay on top of how you look and feel. I constantly try to look my best, even

when I don't feel like it. Like when I don't want to work out because I'm too tired. Or when eating healthy takes too much time and energy. But I know that if I neglect my body, I'll pay for it. My health, my skin, and my confidence will all go south. So I push through the struggle to take care of myself. Examples include:
1. Plan to have your gym bag or a healthy lunch ready to go the night before.
2. Wake up early before the family to meditate, eat breakfast or exercise.
3. Find an hour of time during the day just for you.

Try, try, and try to take out 20-45 minutes, at least three times a week, to exercise. Be creative with it. I like to work out with girlfriends because we're a support system for each other, holding one another accountable. I also like to try different aerobic or weight lifting classes like cardio kick boxing, instead of the routine treadmill or water aerobics. In the summer and spring, I enjoy taking walks or bike riding with my children and husband in the neighborhood or around the lake. That way I kill two birds with one stone; I am exercising and modeling healthy habits while spending time and bonding with my family.

Doing chores around the house are excellent ways of exercising. As mothers, I am sure we get our fair share of exercising around the house doing the job we love the most- cleaning! Cleaning the house helps you to "get moving", burning calories all while beautifying the place. Examples include:
1. Gardening - I have grown to love planting annuals and perennials in the spring. Not only does the yard look beautiful but can also be a very peaceful and therapeutic activity that you can do while children are napping or away.
2. Clearing out the clutter - De cluttering closets, a basement or garage is a great way to get rid of waste,

providing a more peaceful, organized environment for you and family. You could also turn the de-cluttering project into orchestrating an annual garage sale.
3. Sprucing up the house through: painting, moving furniture around, new pictures, fresh flowers or other mementoes giving your house the home feel.

When you exercise and eat healthy with your children, you not only feel better but you are teaching them that it's important for Mom to take care of herself. Then they see self-care as something important that they can carry on within their own lives as well.

Staying fit gives you way more stamina and energy for those lovemaking sessions with that hubby of yours. I guarantee you that he will thank God and whatever other forces that got you motivated to start taking better care of yourself (not that some of us care). And believe it or not, lovemaking sessions are also a way of getting in some good physical exercise. After four kids, I personally don't feel like putting a lot of effort in for those lovemaking sessions but whenever I get just a flash of "the feeling" I go for it with the hubby. I don't even worry about being in a romantic setting or looking va va voomish. I just go for it. If I don't, it will never happen. Please tell your husband not to thank me too much for this piece of advice. Seriously though, if you can find time when the children are asleep, or can schedule, yes, schedule in at least one day a week when you two can "get it going", you will reap a harvest of benefits.

According to the Stanford Daily the top 10 secret health benefits of sex are:
1. Helps you live longer.
2. Strengthens your heart.
3. Reduces stress and depression.
4. Strengthens bones and muscles.
5. Improves your memory and keeps your mind sharp.
6. Helps you look younger.

7. Improves your sense of smell.
8. Provides pain relief.
9. May reduce the risk of prostate cancer
10. Boosts the immune system.

Wow! Who would have known you could get all of that from a couple of scheduled lovemaking sessions with the hubby! I know I could personally stand to work on # 5, and continue working on #6!
And one more thing: to look great and feel good, do not compare yourself to other women. Chances are that same woman is doing the same thing right back at you. The key to looking fabulous is to work with what you got, take care of it and even flaunt it a little. Step out the box and try a new color or style of clothing that compliments and accentuates your figure. I know I have skinny legs, but I have a great upper body so I accentuate that by wearing blouses that show off my arms and collarbone area. Now when I say flaunt it, don't go overboard by wearing those spandex pants with that too short shirt because you think that your behind is your best asset. Or don't stuff yourself into that shirt that is way too tight around your chest and mid-section, letting it all hang out, and embarrassing your children. I'm saying to accentuate what you have, in a nice but classy way which may give you that extra fabulous boost needed to keep it movin' through the day. Overall ladies, between meditating, exercising and lovemaking you will feel fabulous, look fabulous and have more confidence in yourself.

C.) Your Spirit - Connect to it!
Your spirit is your inner being and self, and the connection between you and God. And your spirit within hungers to be awakened and nourished just like your mind and body! Not taking care of your spirit leaves you restless and unfulfilled like your life has no real sense of direction, guidance or purpose. If you are experiencing any of those feelings you

need to take out the time to sit, be quiet and get in tune with your spirit so you can be a more sane and effective mom, wife, and person.

So how can you become more in tune with your spirit? Set aside time each day for prayer, reflection, and spiritual reading. Taking care of your spirit may help you to be more perceptive, patient and rational when dealing with your children, husband, and life's challenges. Praying and reading the bible gives me a clearer perspective on how to handle the stressors in my life. I am more patient, loving and appreciative of what God has blessed me with after I've prayed. Devotional time allows me to love my family all the more and makes me want to make a difference in other's lives as well. Developing love between you and God also deepens the love you will have for yourself and for others.

I know you're thinking. "How am I supposed to find time in my hectic day to pray and get in tune with my spirit?" One step at a time, one day at a time. And build up to a regular regime of spirit care.

Find a time to combine all three – mind, body, and spirit - on a daily basis. You can stop and breathe and pray wherever you are. You can make time in the car driving those kids around, at work during your lunch hour, or in the house while you're cleaning up. Go to the gym to exercise and while you're on the treadmill, listen to music that may encourage you and pumps you up, or read something that enlightens you. After the workout you may relax in the steam room and meditate and pray to God. Give thanks and appreciate what you have in your life. Oh, how much better you will feel leaving the gym compared to how you felt walking in. Disciplining yourself to go to the gym allows you to take care of all three parts of yourself - mind, body and spirit - while the kids are with a sitter or in the gym day-care. Making room for your spirit to grow also guides and leads you when making life decisions or even smaller daily ones. Life becomes more meaningful and rich when you take out time to connect with your inner spirit.

Here are some examples from my life that show how connecting with your spirituality can help you to lead a more meaningful life.

There were specific times in my life when I felt depressed, because I felt I wasn't doing enough in my life by a certain age. At thirty, I had acquired a graduate degree and two undergraduate degrees but still felt unfulfilled. I accomplished those goals as a single mother raising a daughter while working a full-time job. I had also accomplished other goals that I had set out to accomplish in my life but yet again, felt restless and unsatisfied. I have stressed myself out to the max trying to figure out how I am going to "come up in life". When is my big break going to come? When am I going to get that perfect job that I've been praying and working for? I told others about my many and plenty ideas of the next big thing. Many of my ideas did not happen because either my heart was not truly there or because God didn't have that particular plan for me. Through it all, I learned that I have to be still and connect with my inner spirit to hear from God. Connecting to my inner spirit allows me to feel revived and alive. To know that I don't have to constantly search for my purpose in life because God has it already figured out if I just trust Him and be still. I'm still learning to be still!

The biggest moment when I felt like God made me sit down and be still was when I found out I was pregnant again. I already had a 10-year-old daughter and a 19-month-old son that I had just stopped nursing a month prior. Even though my husband and I discussed having a third child (biologically this baby would be his second) because we wanted more children and wanted our second child to have a playmate, I was crushed when I found out that I was pregnant. I was at a point in my life when things were coming together for me. I was movin' in a new direction with my career, going from education into music. Being pregnant felt like my dream was being taken away. I would have to start all over again with another baby. And then I found out at a routine 5-month ultrasound that I wasn't only pregnant with one baby but I was pregnant with two! I lost it. I was in shock and crying, telling the ultrasound technician that I couldn't have four babies. That period of time was one of the toughest times of my life.

I was utterly sick for eight months carrying the twins. I took prescription medicine to prevent vomiting every day. I had everything from sinus infections to the flu to preeclampsia. Preeclampsia is a condition that women carrying multiples run the risk of having, and one symptom is high blood pressure. This was discovered at my eight-month ultra sound exam. It was then that the doctors told me that I would have to be induced or risk the chances of having a stroke.

The hospital was a whole other trial that I had to deal with. The communication process between the nurses, the doctors and the laboratory after I was induced was ineffective and the procedures were not handled in the correct order. As a result I received the epidural way too late after being induced. I continually told the nurse and anesthesiologist that my son was coming, but they wouldn't listen and injected the epidural needle down my back anyway.

If it weren't for the Lord, I would have hurt everyone in the room. I kept saying, "I can do all things through Christ", so I would not curse and slap everyone.

After I managed to get the epidural needle, I was told to lie down. It was then that my son began to come out. "He's coming", I yelled as they continued not to listen. Finally they checked me and realized that what I said was indeed true. I was rushed out into the hallway, with five people all around me. Everything was spinning. I was in excruciating pain (the epidural didn't work because I received it too late) and I was Screaming, "He's Coming, Now!" Then the most humiliating and painful thing happened. My son came whooshing out of me in the hallway on the bed, in front of a lady getting ice at the ice machine. After delivering my son in the hallway, I was wheeled to the operating room to deliver my daughter vaginally. I waited twenty more minutes to push my daughter out. Mind you, I gave birth to twins without any pain medication, with preeclampsia, and hooked up to an IV for this horribly, sickening medication. The last straw was when I went home from the hospital with the IV still in my arm and had to return to the hospital to have it taken out!

After being discharged from the hospital, I decided to go back and stay three more nights in the special nursery to care for my premature babies and nurse them around the clock. They stayed an additional week and a half in order to feed on their own and gain enough weight to be discharged. How exhausted I was.

One day I had to bring my two-year-old son, who is asthmatic, with me to the hospital. While I was trying to nurse both babies, my son had an asthma attack so I had to leave the babies at the hospital to take my two- year-old to the urgent care clinic to receive treatment. Then I had to get back to the hospital, an hour later, to nurse the twins again! In spite of it all, thank God, I brought home two beautiful, healthy babies, a boy and a girl.

But my struggle wasn't over. Reality kicked in when the twins came home and I fully realized that I now had four kids. One who was asthmatic and had to be taken into the hospital for prednisone, (for asthma attacks) once a month for five months straight prior to the birth of the twins. My oldest daughter was actively involved in several activities and reaching puberty at a time when she really needed my attention. And now I was responsible for two other lives, two new babies who also needed to be loved and cared for.

My marriage was also challenged, along with my mind and body. I, being superwoman, decided to nurse both the twins since I had done it with my older children. However, it wouldn't have been right if I didn't have problems nursing as well. After all, carrying the children was quite a feat, along with the difficult labor and delivery, so having minor complications trying to feed them should go with the territory, right? Right. I found out at their two-month checkup that they had developed thrush or yeast in their mouths, and of course, I had it too. I experienced continuous shooting pains in my breast, and was in terrible pain when I tried to pump milk or nurse. I also had a milk flow problem on my left side, so I had to just feed them on my right breast.

I found myself thinking Lord; can I just have a break? Not nursing the twins, like I did my other children, made me feel like a bit of a failure. However, after a bit of prayer and a lot of baby formula, I quickly got over that feeling. I realized that as long as they got some milk from me, it was better than none.

No matter what I had wanted for my pregnancy, birth, nursing and raising my babies, God had another plan for me. Naturally I continued to struggle, but I had to surrender to whatever God had in store for me. I knew, deep down inside, that the twins, along with my other children, were definitely a blessing. If it wasn't for my spiritual relationship with God, my husband and my mother, I don't know if I could have made it through.

I found peace through prayer, searching for scriptures that pertained to my life, singing praises to God and writing. Challenges in your life can be turned into blessings if you're able to overcome them or find the positive within them. Of course carrying the twins was a blessing, but I honestly didn't feel that way at all times. I knew that I had to do something else to pick up my spirits. It was during those tough times that I became motivated to write this book and began to transition into another phase of my life. I knew that writing would unleash my inner creativity and help me to produce something else that I could control and be proud of besides the twins and my other children. Praying and writing has been a form of therapy and healing when I've been through dark periods in my life. They have both given me a sense of inner peace and joy.

Beyond the writing, I knew that I had no other choice but

to get in tune with the spirit of God. It is in those moments where I find strength when I am weak and contentment when I am restless. I feel everlasting joy when I am depressed and peace when I feel overwhelmed. It was also during those times that I began to work on turning my dreams into a reality. I am continuously seeking ways to grow within many aspects of my life. I feel alive when revelation takes place through my spiritual life and the word. I thrive best in relationships where I grow in knowledge from a person and vice versa. I love to be surrounded by conscious music, the arts, positive people, conversation, justice, and environments where I can be a blessing. When I am in tune with the spirit, I am a more sane and effective mom, wife, and person. Try it for yourself.

Reflection Time - What are some things I could do to take better care of me?
Okay, I am not promising anything because I know what happens when I make promises that I don't keep. I may give up entirely or feel that I let myself down. And I don't need to give up or feel bad. So I am going to try, try, try to take better care of my mind and I want to:

I also want to try, try, try to take care of my body, so I will squeeze in some exercise, in a creative way, for at least_____ minutes, three times a week. I will:

If I am unable to get in my three weekly workouts or lovemaking sessions (I thought I'd sneak that one in) then I'll count doing the laundry, picking up after the little and big people in the house and walking up and down the stairs to use the bathroom as at least 3 weekly workout sessions. On a more serious note, in order to renew my spirit, I will take out at least_____minutes a day to sit down and:

By doing this I do believe it will help me:

You know you're a Mother when:

- Your idea of a vacation is being locked in the bathroom with the faucet running!

- The only weights you're lifting are groceries and twenty pound kids.

- You haven't noticed that you've been wearing the same shirt for three days until your child points it out to you.

Step 2
Be True to Who You Are! Aside from Being a Mom and a Wife

Who are you? Who were you before you became a mother and wife? Can you remember? If your life was a fairy tale, and anything was possible, without any distractions or obstacles, what are some goals you would like to accomplish? As human beings we are all constantly changing but the very core of your being is the same as it ever was.

So how can you discover who your true self is outside of motherhood and all the other titles you carry? Set aside a few minutes within the day for self reflection, to get better acquainted with yourself again. (This can happen when you are also taking the time out to pray or meditate.) Start by telling yourself, out loud, (just don't talk back) positive messages. Some messages I say to myself are: I am beautiful, I am happy, I am blessed, I love myself, I will succeed! Words are so powerful. You'll be amazed at how you feel about yourself or your outlook on life if you just open up your mouth to speak things into existence. The more you speak it, the more you believe it, and the more you will become your true self.

An exercise you can do to remember who you are is to

think back to when you were a child; hopefully you can remember some good times. What made you happy then? What did you enjoy doing? What did you not get enough of? For example: I wrote in my diary a lot and made up songs and sang them for my family, and acted goofy around the house. I also auditioned for a lot of plays. Never got a part, but I didn't let that stop me from trying. Taking time to remember what I loved doing as a child helped me to realize dreams of being a performer before adulthood kicked in.

Try writing to remind yourself who you were before motherhood, the husband and all the expectations heaped on you from friends and relatives. Through writing, prayer and self-reflection, you can find your core. For instance here's what I've learned about myself:

I am most passionate when I am utilizing the gifts that God has given me to bless and inspire others.

I can be a fabulous mother and wife and still work hard at reaching my dreams as well.

It's important to reinvent myself as a writer, singer and speaker.

I have a voice to speak out against injustice while educating others.

My work is something that I do but not who I am.

I am inspired through the art of music, dance, theatre, and poetry.

It's okay to just be me, not caring what anyone else thinks as long as my family and I are happy and well.

I am free to be me, all of me. It took some time to get here but now that I am here, I am not going to let it go. Trying to be something or someone I am not just makes me unhappy.

I found out about my true self and you can too by writing in your journal and spending time in self-reflection.

Here are some simple truths that can help you be who you really are:

1. You don't have to be anybody but yourself. In the past I thought if only I could sing like this person, I would really go far, or if I had that person's gift I would... I had to discover my unique gifts and accept that I am who I am and I have plenty of positive attributes to share with the world.
2. You can't depend on anyone to make you happy or complete. In order to be whole you have to work on self and have an outlet outside of family. Otherwise you may lose yourself.
3. Do not let anybody tell you who you are. If you are around someone who is constantly trying to change you and or bring you down through words or abuse - get away from them. If you don't, you may wake up one day, not knowing who you are, where you are or how you got there. You have to know who you are first, that is how you remain true to yourself.
4. Creating your own happiness and destiny is important.

For example, if you know that your husband or children are slow at making plans for your birthday or for Mother's Day and you like to do something special to celebrate, you can take it upon yourself to make plans. You could tell them what you want to do instead of complaining about it. This way you won't be disappointed when your special day arrives. I have no problems with planning my own birthday or mother's day plans. I simply suggest a place to my hubby and he goes to work. It's a win, win situation. He doesn't have to play the guessing game of what to do and I don't have to be disappointed when the day arrives. I also love to travel, instead of complaining or waiting on my hubby to take me, I may spontaneously fly somewhere inexpensive to get away and relax, venturing off into a new world. Like on my birthday, my husband and best girlfriends helped me pull off a dream birthday getaway to Miami because they knew that's what I wanted!

I spent four blissful days there, taking care of only myself. It was exhilarating. I appreciated every moment and was so glad that I spoke up.

Here is an entry from my journal that might illuminate how you can write to get clear about who you are.

Who AM I?

Who am I? Who is Christine? I am passionate, a free spirit, a child of God. I am complex. I love to sing, to write, to speak about something inspirational, in depth, justice. I love to help others through words, or action to utilize the various gifts that God has blessed me with, igniting my passions. I am a mother, a wife, a daughter, a sister, and a friend to many.

Who am I? I am confident. I am strong, I am sexy and beautiful. I am loved. I am successful. I am. I am a successful mother, a homemaker, a leader at church, in my community. I am blessed and destined to succeed, to continue to rise up to the top for I truly know that I can do all things through Christ that strengthens me!

Reflection Time - My True Self

I am_____(adjective) and I love to _____

(verb) because it makes me feel_____(adjective).

My close friends would describe me as a_____

(adjective) person because I_____(verb). Society

has told me that mothers or women aren't supposed

to_____but deep down I've always felt_____

and_____wanted_____to_____I am going to

start listening to my inner self. Believing that it's okay to be

_____.

I just need to be me, just me, not someone else or what someone else expects me to be. Being true to myself is where happiness lies.
1. Ask yourself these questions as well:
2. Who are you outside of a being a mother and a wife?
3. When you look in the mirror what do you see?
4. How do you feel about yourself?
5. If you were stripped of all titles, who would you be?
6. Are you happy being alone with just yourself without anyone else around, without any distractions and noise?
7. Are you happy with your life? Why or why not?
8. What inspires and motivates you?
9. What talents do you possess?
10. What would you change about your life to feel happy or fulfilled?

If you are having a hard time answering these questions, don't worry, it may mean you just need to take time out for some self-reflection. Answering them might be an ongoing process as more of your inner self is revealed to you. Use these questions to get you started and also come up with lots of different questions to ask yourself in order to get to know yourself. Look over your answers and see what you can find out about who you really are.

If you don't like what you come up with, like maybe you find that you don't have the highest self-esteem, pray and seek out wise counsel from a positive person like your husband, girlfriend or mentor until you get there. Outside of my husband, my cousin and girlfriends constantly challenges me to step out and explore my dreams. My cousin believed in me and my talents even when I didn't totally believe in myself. She affirmed what I felt inside until I began to say it, believe it and act upon it. My daughter and niece are also a great sound board for trying out new music that I may be working on. Because they are so young, they have no problem being honest with me as to whether they think the song is a thumb's up or down and what I can do to make it better. However, the best way I have been able to believe in myself took place through writing in my journal, prayer and time alone. Discovering your true self is a journey. Be patient with yourself. You'll get there.

You know you're a Mother when:

- Your idea of rest happens when you're at work, away from the house and children.

- You have to give yourself a "time-out".

- Lovemaking happens while you're napping and you wake up and ask your husband "Are you done yet?"

Step 3
Dare to Dream! And Find Your Passion

Are you living your dream? I don't mean the kind of dream where your hubby and children clean up after themselves or the one where your husband brings you roses and massages your back on your command! Nah, ladies, that's something we'll get to later in the book. What I'm talking about is something that you've always wanted to do. Something you're passionate up about. Maybe it's a class or field of study that you want to take, or a new skill that you want to learn. Maybe you want to travel to a new place or start that part-time business or help other people out in some way that only you can. Whatever your dream is, dare to do it!

When I graduated from high school I had a dream of attending Clark Atlanta University. Originally from Minneapolis, Minnesota, I wanted to change environments and attend a Historically Black College in the south. The odds were against me. I didn't get accepted right out of high school. As a result I stayed in Minnesota and went to Concordia College University for two years until I brought my grade point average up. I worked hard during those two years making sure to take classes I knew would transfer to Clark. When I finally was accepted, I moved 1,130 miles away from my very close-knit family relying solely on financial aid and a small scholarship. The people in my life at the time doubted that I would be able to pull it off. After all, I was the first person in my immediate and extended family to go to college alone as a sophomore. But what they didn't know was that, even though, I was only twenty years old, I had a concrete plan, a lot of faith, and a dream to journey outside of Minneapolis to graduate from a Historically Black College.

I transferred to Clark in my sophomore year, with eighty dollars to my name, and a big dream to tackle. That was during the early 90's when cell phones were not a commodity so I relied solely on pay phones to communicate to family. I braved the twenty-four hour drive to Atlanta alone, thinking, several times, that I would die because of the deep fears I had to conquer. This was the first time I ever drove long distance and used a map. I'm deathly afraid of heights and had to drive over bridges, and through mountain ranges on my 1,130 mile trip. Once I saw the sign that said 'Welcome To Atlanta', I felt a surge of energy rush through my body. I made it and nothing could stop me now. Or so I thought. I was physically exhausted from the twenty-four hour car ride so I got sick right off the bat. And during my three-year stay in Atlanta I was robbed, wrongfully arrested and became an unwed mother at the age of 23.

I could have easily given up chasing my dream but my faith in God and my ambition wouldn't allow me to do so. The thought of returning to Minnesota without accomplishing what I set out to do made me shudder. It wasn't just about me. I had to prove to myself and others that if I could do it, they could do it as well. I held on and worked harder than I had ever worked in my life at the time. At one point, I was a full time student and worked two part time jobs all while keeping my grades up. In my senior year I gave birth to a beautiful baby girl and was involved with her father for several years afterward. Again, I could have easily thrown in the towel, but my faith kept me movin' upward. Two and a half years later after arriving in Atlanta, I walked across the stage with the diploma in my hand from Clark Atlanta University. My six-month-old daughter, family members and friends were in the audience to congratulate and support me.

That's just one example of the challenges you may have to go through to reach your dream. If you stay focused and determined, you'll be surprised what you'll be able to do to overcome the difficulties and obstacles in your life.

You're never too old to make your dreams come true. And your dreams can change at any point of your life. It took me a long time to know and understand my purpose in life. I now know through prayer, writing, struggles, joys, and the birth of my children what my purpose is and my dreams.

Each time I gave birth to a child it felt like I was also giving birth to a new dream. With my oldest daughter came the dream of continuing on with my education even though I had some challenges and would have to work harder to obtain the educational degrees. With the birth of my second child came the gift of writing songs. My dad is a songwriter and poet. As a child I would make up songs quite often, however I didn't believe I had the gift to do so until I was pregnant with my second child. I began to write songs and would sing them to others who loved the songs and felt I had the gift to write, so I continued on writing songs. With the twins came the ability and dream to write this book, which I felt ultimately gave me the voice and platform to tie all the dreams together of writing, singing and speaking to inspire others.

I went into education because people told me that I would be a great teacher or administrator. It was a safe route for me to go, being that I was unmarried with a daughter. So I pushed my dreams of becoming an aspiring actress or singer and set out to obtain a second undergraduate degree in k-8 education as well as a graduate degree in education. I became a teacher and educator for several years. Only it wasn't that simple. I was good at what I did as a teacher/educator, but my heart was not totally in it. I wasn't content. I was always searching for something other than what I had. To top it off, I had worked very hard to get my second undergraduate degree in k-8 education but couldn't pass a state test to receive the actual teaching license. I was able to teach without a license for a period of time but I felt like I was never really "respected" as a real teacher without that piece of paper. I took that test seven times, getting all the help you can imagine, but I still continued to fail. Now, I am a person that doesn't give up, who keeps trying until I reach my goal, so that was a hard period of time for me. I began to go through this self reflective down time. I saw the redundant story of my life play out, all the reasons why I wasn't as successful as I should be. Finally, a friend told me that maybe God had something else in mind for me. I realized that I had to let go of this test, this life as an educator, if I was to remain sane. I had to come to terms with the idea that there was something else I was supposed to do and move on. I began to transition from the old and familiar into something new. I was constantly saying to myself and writing, "Christine create the life you want. Nobody can make your dreams come true except you. You truly have it within you to do or be whatever you want. Life is about the choices you make." I stepped out on faith and tried something different. I learned that I have choices. I can walk around feeling doomed because my life is not where I want it to be or I can take action and do something about it. And let me tell you, doing something about your life feels much better than walking around feeling doomed.

 Since I was a child, I had been making up songs around the house and singing with my brother and sister in church. My father is a pastor and had been a part of a gospel group with his brothers when I was growing up. My mother too is a singer. She sings often times leading praise and worship or singing lead vocal in the choir. Her voice is absolutely angelic. The world feels like a much better place when I hear my parents sing or when I heard them playing all the gospel greats growing up like Shirley Ceasar, The Winans, or the Clark Sisters. Being a singer was in my bones but as an adult, people only identified me as an educator. And being an educator wasn't making me feel fulfilled about myself these days. I wanted to get back to what I loved. So, I dared to dream. I gave myself a goal of performing outside of the church environment within a year. I signed up for singing classes and went into the studio with my brother-in-law to record an instrumental track that I could perform with. I practiced, a great deal, in my spare time with my brother and my friends. In just two weeks' time, I got the nerve to perform on stage. And so in the summer of 2008, I got on stage in front of all my family and friends and I sang two of my songs (a cross between neo-soul and inspirational). It was a dream come true. I was transitioning from the "great educator" to the "singer, song writer". I was given the opportunity and I seized the moment. I got great feedback. Many people told me that they wouldn't have had the nerve or drive to do what I did. It felt fabulous.

Let me also say you that I've learned as a mother of four that you have to adopt a "just do it" attitude. I can't wait for the right time, that will never happen. I just have to do it. I may be tired and beat to the bones but "just doing it" again refuels me to keep it movin'. When the twins were a year and a half, I kept it movin' by auditioning for a film in Atlanta, was the director of a district choir, sung and took part in a weekend choir workshop and networked at several events and meetings. I can honestly say that within all those environments I may have felt uncomfortable or initially to exhausted to go. However, afterwards I always felt satisfaction from the experience because it was for me and I learned something each situation. Whatever your dream is, take some time out to see exactly what's stopping you from getting there. Dare to dream big! Take your opportunity and go for it.

Throughout your life you may have several dreams that change as time goes on. Maybe you wanted to be a nurse, at one point, but then changed your mind because you found out later that you're really passionate about acting. Many dreams can come true. You can accomplish one dream in a certain time frame and then begin pursuing a new one. Your dream could take place in a day or over a lifetime. Here are a few suggestions that I have found helpful along the way regarding your dreams:

A.) Believe in Yourself
You have to believe in yourself. Pray it out, practice it out, chant it out, write it out, or sing it out. Do whatever it takes to build up your confidence.

B.) Visualize it!
When you begin to believe that you can totally do it, visualize yourself doing it or being it. For example, even though I was already a teacher, I could see myself being a singer (outside of church) whether I was the backup or lead. I could also see myself as a writer. In both scenarios my main purpose was to inspire and that's what I am doing!

C.) Be careful who you share your dreams with!
There are a lot of haters and doubters out there. People who can't stand to see anyone succeed because they are miserable with their own lives or lack the faith, ambition, or courage to make a change. Tell only supportive, positive people in your life who will offer you encouragement, feedback and support.

D.) Girlfriend, plan on how you're going to get there!
A dream without a plan is just that, a dream. What will it take for you to accomplish your dream? What do you need to go forth with the dream? Know that some dreams may take more time and planning than others but if you have a plan and stay focused, you'll get there. Create attainable baby steps for yourself that will get you closer to your main goal. What are the roadblocks that stop you from accomplishing the dream? How will you overcome them? Make a plan through writing

out specific goals and steps, building a support system of people and resources and sticking to it.

E.) Don't Talk about It Be About It!
Nothing will happen in your life if you're not willing to put the plan into action. Yes, doing so will take a lot of hard work, perseverance, and dedication, but in the end it will have all been worth it. Trying to find time and energy to work on my dreams is extremely challenging with four kids but I have to do it. I may wake up at 3 a.m. after feeding one of the twins to write that song down, or work on this book. As I've stated earlier there are plenty of times that I don't feel like taking time to plan or work but if I don't my dreams will never happen. I am a big believer of the scripture; "Faith Without Works is Dead." (James 2:14) Don't talk about it, be about it!

Reflection Time - Dare to Dream and Find your Passion
Use this road map to figure out your dreams, purpose, or gifts. If I could do anything in the world besides what I am doing now it would be:

I feel the most inspired and passionate when I am:

Even if I wasn't getting paid I would continue to:

42 Nurturing the Inner Me

People have told me that I have a gift for:

Here are three steps and flexible time lines that I will take to get there:

Step One:

Time line to get there:

Step Two:

Time line to get there:

Step Three:

Time line to get there:

So, again ladies, take the time to unleash your inner dreams, knowing that anything is possible if you believe and work to make it happen.

You know you're a Mother when:

- Your idea of a great massage is having your child step on your back with her shoes on.

- Your "alone time" is spent hiding in your closet, holding your breath, praying no one hears you.

- You hear your single girlfriends talking about their dates, their days, and their adventures and it's as if they're speaking a foreign language!

Step 4
Slow Down, Breathe and Relax!

Ladies, have you ever had a moment when you had so much on your mind that you forgot what you called someone for? Or maybe you rushed out of the house, carrying your son, stubbed your toe, and dropped all your things (not the baby, thank God) on the ground. You're just trying to get to the car and your day hasn't even begun!!! What about those times when you know you put the keys in a certain spot but just can't find them and you have to be somewhere in 20 minutes, which is when your child decides to push your buttons the most. Oh, The Pressure, The Pressure, The Pressure!

It is times like those when you have to Slow Down, Breathe, and Relax! If you don't, you might just snap out and do something extreme, like run away and take a vacation that you can't afford. (I may have done that…). Or drive to the mall and charge those designer shoes and handbags, one in every color, to your husband's account (yeah right, what a dream.) You definitely don't need to go overboard like that, now do you?

Instead, take just a minute or two to stop, and breathe. In moments of chaos you may have to just sit down for a moment to regain focus and evaluate the situation. It won't cost you a thing and when you take the time to center yourself you are able to make a different choice. Like, I've come to grips with the fact that I may get my daughter to school a few minutes late, but that's better than getting her there on time and upset from me snapping or driving reckless. When you calm down enough to think you get a clearer perspective on things.

It pays to always plan ahead, you won't have to rush or to be ultra organized, you won't misplace things that lead to major frustration in a critical moment. But as much as we all try, no one lives in a perfect world. Just know that you will misplace things and there will be moments of "hurriedness" but you can always get through those times if you just Slow Down and Breathe.

And on top of slowing down and breathing find ways to relax on a weekly basis. One of my latest relaxation methods has been going to my community coffee shop or local bar/restaurant, all by myself. If I don't leave my house, I start cleaning or tending to the kids, and I don't get any time to relax. I usually go for one or two hours in the evening when my husband is available to be there for the children or I will hire a sitter. I feel so exhilarated while I am there and refreshed when I leave. I usually order a glass of wine or coffee, depending on where I'm at, and work on a song or write in my journal about whatever my heart desires. Alone and out in the world like this I am able to reinvent myself, to transition from the reliable mommy, wife, educator, girl in the box and transform into the "other Christine" -the passionate, inspired, singer, writer, in-depth, sexy, free-spirited, dreamer Christine! Taking time out during the week, to breathe, relax, let go and create your own moments is essential to feeling refueled.

Another way I found to relax and let go was taking a trip without the hubby and kids. I felt a bit uneasy about it at first, but after receiving support from my hubby and family to do so, I ran at the chance. The twins were 6 months old and the other children were 2 and 11. I flew for the first time in a bazillion years without a child. Wow, how totally exciting and relaxing that was. I had decided that I would however make it a working, fun trip. I wrote down a few things that I wanted to accomplish in Atlanta while I was there visiting family and friends. I wanted to continue working on this book, to find a place somewhere that I could get on stage to be free and sing a few songs I wrote. I wrote the goals out for the trip and I accomplished all three. It was fabulous! I began writing a new song on the way to Atlanta on the plane. I sat next to a nice man that wanted to tell me all about his business of selling barn kits while I was writing. The information you discover about others when you're traveling alone without a kid is amazing. I also got the courage to find a soulful night café where I was able to go on stage during an open microphone event for aspiring artists where I was able to sing. What a rush that was! After I performed I was approached by the owner of the cafe to send him my CD! In addition, I worked on completing this book. I had a wonderful time and was able to get a ton of things done that I wouldn't have been able to do within those three days if I was at home with my lovely children and hubby.

- Now a trip is big but there are small ways to relax and feel rejuvenated. Here is a list of quick suggestions from myself and other mothers: Light a candle, and read a couple pages of a book – this book would be good.
- Buy a great shower head and take an indulging shower or a shower/bath- where you put the stopper in the tub and let it steam in and block out the noise.
- Talk to a big person who will listen and can relate to you.
- Force yourself to find a sitter for an hour and half to make a date night with your hubby.
- Drop the children off at the sitter's, with a relative, or at an hourly childcare center, so you can nap or play.
- Put the kids to bed early so you can have the night to yourself.

- If your kids are old enough, have them go outside on a nature scavenger hunt. Choose 5 to 7 things that they are to collect. The first one to finish gets a prize. The hunt allows you to have some alone time.
- Decorate a room in your house.
- Hang out with girlfriends.
- Take a nice walk, breathe and appreciate the beauty of the outdoors.
- Eat your favorite dessert in the car so you don't have to share it. Indulge all by yourself - you deserve it!
- Go to the bookstore.
- Hole yourself up in your room to watch your favorite series of television shows.
- Do weekly pampering rituals like, getting your hair, nails, or eyebrows done Get a massage or a facial.
- Be a kid again and revisit what used to make you happy and relaxed.
- Lock yourself in the bathroom, pamper yourself or watch a movie on a portable DVD player.
- Get a hotel room for the weekend, by yourself.
- Remind your kids and husband that there is another parent that lives in the house and his name is Daddy.
- Go to the gym and relax in the steam room or sauna while the kids are in the playroom.
- Sign up for that class that you've always wanted to take.
- Go dancing.
- Tickle your kids.
- Have your husband tickle you!
- Rent a comedy - laughter is good for the soul.

Reflection Time - Slow Down, Breathe and Relax!
Taking a few seconds to inhale and exhale in times of "hurriedness" can help clear my mind. Other ways I may overcome moments of "hurriedness" may be to plan ahead For when I have to go:

Or do:

Ways I could learn to relax on a weekly basis could be:

And:

Taking time to slow down, breath and relax could help me to:

You know you're a Mother when:

- Your idea of birth control with your husband is abstinence.

- Your old fragrance of choice used to be Chanel but has been replaced with sweeter fragrances and fluids like baby spit up and others I won't mention!

- Your car looks like a herd of animals ran through it and left it for you to take care of.

Section 2

How to Stay Sane Balancing Family, Kids, Husband, and Work

Step 5
Get Organized - Calendars and Routines Are a Necessity

Okay ladies, we are movin' away from the deep spiritual side of our lives into the lovely, organized and structured part of our lives. We need to consider our sanity. I have found, along with other mothers, when I have a somewhat set routine for myself and my children, things run smoother. Kids, of all ages, as well as husbands thrive when routines are set. The structure gives them a sense of balance and provides stability. When everyone in your house knows what to do or what to expect, during certain times of the day, your family will feel secure and comfortable, making your life a bit easier.

For example, If you know your child has to have a nap between 1:00 and 3:00, plan on being home between those times or you could instruct the nanny (what a luxury) to make that happen everyday. If you don't, you might as well get ready to deal with the repercussions, like all the whining and tantrums, which will leave you feeling as if the end of the world is here. If you are a stay-at-home mother, structured nap time is a great way to have some "me time" to do for yourself or if you dare - your home. If you are an out-of-the-house-working mom you may have to adjust the "me time" schedule. I decided to have the nerve to take on a job as a kindergarten teacher when the twins were 18 months old. I was able to get me time early in the morning before work or never. After work I was way too exhausted to think or do anything else besides being with the kids and the usual chores.

Suggested times to have a set routine in place:
- Dinner time - it's a great way for children to help out, and a good way to bond with them and your hubby.
- Homework time - for older children. I have placed the expectation on my daughter to get a snack and do her homework everyday (without the television on) as soon as she gets home from school or from an extracurricular activity.
- Bedtime for small children and older children, when you can. Having a routine bed time works well for you and the child's peace of mind! For my younger one, I turn on his lullaby music at 8:00 p.m. and repeatedly tell him its night, night, time. Either my husband or I give him a bath, get his pajamas on, read him a story, rock him a few times in the rocking chair, say his prayers and put him in his bed. I know that sounds like a lot of work. It can take around 30 minutes and believe me; we don't necessarily do all that every night, either. Some nights he's good to just get his pajamas on and a sippy cup! But the point is that it works. My son knows what to expect every night since he was one year old. If I have any energy left, I have the night to myself or to spend with my husband. Yippee! With my 10-year-old, I tell her repeatedly at 8:00 p.m. to set her clothes out and take her bath before 8:45, so she can be in bed by 9:00. Of course, it doesn't work as well with her now that she's ten but she knows what to expect as well.

- Chore time - for all the children and the hubby. Chores teach everyone in the house to take part and to be responsible. It may be once a week you have the big overall cleaning. Or daily, where your child is expected to do something miraculous like set the table for dinner, pick up after herself, clean his room, or wash the dishes. If you're super organized, I heard of a family creating a weekly chore wheel or chart that is placed in the kitchen. The wheel chart has everyone's chores and names written on pieces the shape of triangles. Eventually I'd like to try that idea, but for now I just write the chores out for my daughter and put it on the refrigerator. Or repeatedly tell her what needs to be done. Yes, if you haven't already set up this routine, be prepared for a lot of Complaining and Whining from children and possibly hubby, alike. Just simply ignore the whining and enforce!

Calendars and planners are a necessity for keeping your family on track and somewhat organized in your daily lives. If I don't have a planner/calendar to remind me of everyone's appointments, I am lost and out of touch with the world. I also like to sit down with my calendar/planner to set up fun activities and events for all of us, play dates for the children or time I can spend with my hubby and my friends. I have to put it in the calendar, otherwise the days and weeks go by so fast that you can't keep track of it all or do any of the things you need or want to do.

If you're one of those high-tech moms that I am not, you probably use your Blackberry or some other technological mystery to keep track of your life. Myself, still being a bit old fashioned and prehistoric, prefer a simple, inexpensive calendar and planner that you can pick up at the drugstore or my favorite therapy store, Target.

Keeping a calendar and planner has also helped me tremendously with mapping out steps towards making my dreams a reality. I may set appointments and reminders in my planner on a weekly basis to work on my writing or music. If I don't, again it'll never happen. Once I finished writing this book I wrote down the steps that it will take to get it published. I gave myself a three month deadline for that process to happen. I also had a backup plan if my first choice of a publisher did not work. During the three months I wrote down what I would have to do to market myself as a writer and singer. I had to transition from being only viewed as an educator to an artist.

Steps for my book included:
1. Send my manuscript to editor for corrections
2. Make changes to book
3. Research editors/publishing companies
4. Send cover letter/portfolio to publishers

Steps for my music included:
1. Work on writing my own songs
2. Organize song list
3. Create a brand for myself as-Christine FREE
4. Network with other artists
5. Get out there and hustle to perform at different venues, church's, café's, etc.
6. Record my songs in the studio.

I also gave myself three months to market myself more-so than I had done in the past as a new author and singer. I joined several website groups to do so. I barely knew how to use them but that didn't stop me from trying. Facebook, twitter, twitter moms, meetup.com, etc. are a few websites I thought I'd be apart of to market myself and seek support. I started a group called Fabulous Moms with a Dream to meet with other moms to get ideas for this book and market myself.

Let me also say that I was working with a very strict budget of almost nothing to make this all happen. So I was dreaming really big. I knew however that if I can get my music and book organized and polished in a portfolio I could talk myself up good to investors and others interested. After all, I now believe in myself and the talents that I possess and have the gift of gab to try and make others believe as well. Ask yourself, what are a few steps that you may have to write down and take to make your dreams a reality?

Clean out your clutter and get rid of what you don't need to stay organized and clear minded. Periodically, I get organized by cleaning out my desk, basement or various other parts of the house, and it leaves me feeling more at peace and balanced.

Connect to your Spiritual Base. If I go days or weeks without praying or reading the bible my life as a whole becomes chaotic and out of order whether I have a planner or not. So it's important for me to check in and connect with God, doing so keeps me ultimately sane and organized.

Reflection Time - Get Organized!
Warning! This may be more fun writing down than enforcing but remember, "Ignore and enforce". Routines that I could try to have my family get into the habit of doing are:

I am going to either be creative or enforce routine 1 by:

I am going to either be creative or enforce routine 2 by:

Something I could use to help make my life organized is:

Steps I could write down towards making my dream a reality is:

You know you're a Mother when:

- Your new lip gloss is Vaseline.

- You now enjoy singing along to the "Wheels on the Bus" and "Old McDonald had a Farm" CD because that's all you can listen to in the car.

- You reach in your purse to get your make up pouch and pull out a diaper instead.

Step 6
Don't Be Afraid to Ask or Pay for Help, You Can't Do It All! It Takes a Village

Do you sometimes feel overwhelmed or frustrated regarding the responsibilities that come along with motherhood? The children, chores, appointments, homework, sleep deprivation, lack of adult social life. What help could you enlist from others that could make things run smoother within your household? Having a written plan to help you with childcare and chores may help alleviate stressors related to motherhood.

I am a big believer in the old saying "You can't do it all". And living in the twenty-first century, it's definitely okay to ask for or to pay for help. In my younger, naive days I thought I could do it all, but was often times left feeling stressed out and upset. Trying to take care of the children and all the household chores at all times by myself took away from time spent pursuing my dreams and spending time with my husband and family. So through out time and experiences, I grew up and decided that I liked having my sanity as well as looking and feeling fabulous.

If you're a woman that believes she can do it all, then you may want to skip this section. Or if you're a mother who has a hard time asking for help, you may have to practice asking out loud to yourself before you ask for someone's help. Ask yourself what you could use a little help with around the house. Would having someone clean my house twice a month make my life a little bit easier? Yep. Or, what could I do with my time if I had a baby sitter come watch the kids for a couple of hours? The list is endless.

There are many different avenues you can take to receive the kind of help that you need with your children or household.

These are three primary sources:
1. The people who live in your house
    - Enlisting help from family members will depend on the age of the little people and the mental age of the other big person who lives there.
    - Here's how they can help: Weekly chores that you enforce! Refer back to your own reflection list in step five that you had fun writing previously.
2. Relatives, friends, and community.
    - Inexpensive childcare - have nieces or nephews watch your children for a couple hours at a wonderfully inexpensive rate!
    - Free Childcare - have your mother or mother-in-law watch the children for a couple of hours at an even greater inexpensive rate - Free!
    - Childcare without strings - have your husband or child's father watch your children at a great inexpensive free rate as well, which is the best of all because you may not have to take them anywhere-just run out the door - Fast!
    - Play date exchanges with my friends' children are another great way to get free childcare and even see your friends.
    - Pay or exchange services with family members or friends that may need work or want to be a blessing by doing household projects like, painting, cleaning, yard work, handy man projects, or day care.

One of the best ideas I came up with for getting good, inexpensive help was when my 13-year-old niece and my daughter were looking for a job to raise money for Christmas presents. I hired them and wrote out four job descriptions so each girl had two jobs a piece. The jobs were:
1. Cleaning the bathroom
2. Organizing all the toy bins and dresser drawers.
3. Sweeping and doing dishes.

The last job was to clean my son's small room. They got paid a whopping $5.00 for each job, totaling $10.00 per girl. They were excited and completed the jobs to my liking. And you know I was beside myself for hiring help at such a great rate. In turn the girls learned lessons on responsibility, hard work and how to earn money. It was a win, win situation. So if you would rather not spend a fortune on help, be creative.

If you do not have a lot of supportive family members or friends to help out, maybe the community you live in has a supportive mom/family group you could join or be a part of. Community centers are a great resource that I have often used. Once or twice a week, I send my son to a local church that has hourly childcare. He's there for three to four hours, depending on if I am working or not. He is able to interact and learn with other children and I am free to either work, fulfill other obligations, or, oh yeah, take care of the twins!

Agencies and referrals are also excellent resources if like me, you don't mind spending the bucks for great help. There are plenty of agencies out there that offer services for anything from baby sitting to cleaning to cooking. I even used a laundry service, before, to do my children's laundry and other items like blankets and sheets. I was criticized by some family members and friends for doing so, but trust me I didn't care! They thought it was a wasteful way to spend money. But they don't live in my house. I say, "Do what you gotta do to stay sane". I do what I need to do to keep my house in order without having to constantly slave away.

If I didn't receive all the help and support from others there would be no way I could have accomplished my dreams of writing, singing and speaking. I had to have someone watch the kids while I left for an hour here or there for myself to write, sing, breath and get refueled. I clean the house everyday but still never have enough time or energy to clean the refrigerator, dust the woodwork or mop the floors, which is what my wonderful cleaning lady does once or twice a month. My motto is if "I am blessed to have the money, I am going bless someone else to do the service." You can't pay enough for great service, well maybe, you know within reason. Since I am such a dreamer, I also have dreams regarding my household. Those dreams include; having a housekeeper come to my home on a weekly basis, having a nanny watch the children a few hours a day while I work or play with my hubby or friends, and having someone help me organize my home life as well! I just feel there are so many other things you can focus your energy on, like enjoying your life and your family and being fabulous in your own way!

Reflection Time - Help Time Yippee!
It would be so nice to receive help with:

My goals or dreams in life like:

Baby sitting on days during hours of_____:

Household chores like:

Sources that I could receive help from are:

Husband and children:

Relatives, friends, community:

Agencies or referrals:

Fill in a source from the list above:

I would like to have_____(who) help me with _____(what) by_____:

If I thought creatively I could receive help by:

You know you're a Mother when:

- When you go play hide and seek and never find your kids.

- When you send your kids to hourly childcare to go to happy hour.

- When you schedule your own daylight savings time to have a early bedtime (set the clock ahead)

Step 7
Make Time for Family, Yeah!

Any way that you do it, raising a family is challenging, so it's important to make time every week to be together. Weekly family time makes you stop, enjoy and appreciate each other all the more and strengthens your family bond. Therefore helping your children feel secure, safe, and included.

I love to see the expression on my kids' faces when my husband and I are taking time out just to be with them. Seeing their smiles, hearing their laughter or watching them learn something new in these moments that we have created is truly priceless. And when they are adults, I'm pretty sure that they will look back on our family times with fondness.

Hard to believe that the focus of my life is not just about me, myself and I, right? But seriously, the "me time" allows me to enjoy the family time even more. So, in addition to all the other things you may do, "being that you are Superwoman", schedule a weekly family day. Your family may share unscheduled moments as well, but trying to schedule family time may help you with consistency. Ideally, one day per week set aside for the family is optimum but sometimes it's hard to fit that in. However, try to make it happen when you can!

Your scheduled family time can fall on Wednesday night. The family could play board games, play with toys or go out to our neighborhood ice cream shop. The kids will love it and really look forward to it.

Other ways you could make family time happen throughout the week is by turning the television off and having even your older children hang out in the family room with the rest of the family. Sometimes my daughter complains about not being able to watch her "important Disney shows", but I know deep down she'll appreciate those moments later on in her life, and if not, oh well! I appreciate them.

Family time is important whether your children are young or old. If your children are older you might come up against some resistance and find that you have to be a bit more creative to get them on board.

Here are some suggestions and tips that other mothers and I have found helpful for creating family time:

1. Talk to your kids about their day when they get out of school.
2. Pick a day of the week where you can have quality family time with your hubby and kids to have game night, pizza night, ice cream social night, etc.
3. If the older kids are in sport games or extracurricular activities have the whole family attend one day a week and trade off weeks with each kid.
4. Turn the television and electronics off. For an hour or two in the evening, force the kids to just read, hang out, or talk in a family room. (Turning the television off even annoys my three year old. He yells, "No Television!" but after a good ten minutes, he's okay.)
5. Take a yearly family vacation.
6. Go to church together.
7. Laugh with your kids and be a kid again for a few moments by:
   - Making a snow angel or a snowman
   - Sledding down the hill
   - Taking family walks
   - Swimming
   - Skating
   - Singing or dancing around the house together

- Bike riding
- Snuggling up, and watching a good movie
- Riding the rides at the local fair or amusement park
- Going to the zoo, seeing and smelling the animals.

And if you want to use your family time to build community, increase your connection to your spirituality and volunteer. This kind of family time can be invaluable creating a sense of love, respect and compassion within your family for God and others. Children look to parents as examples in their lives and learn by parents actions. For instance, my family and I attend church on a regular basis where we are able to interact and bond with extended family members and other people within the church community. My children enjoy participating in various activities at church like Sunday school, children's choir and holiday programs. In Sunday school the children may learn valuable lessons about being respectful, empathetic, and kind individuals.

Being active in the church is also a great way for my husband and I to give back to the community, feeling blessed through our giving of time and efforts in return. I've volunteered as a Sunday school teacher, an assistant choir director, a praise and worship leader and chaired the board of directors. My husband is well respected as the treasurer of the finance board. Our commitment to the church ministry teaches our children the value of blessing others through the gifts that we have been given.

Reflection Time - Family Time
I do believe family time is important. Ways that I could try to incorporate family time within my hectic but blissful week is by simply:

I know that doing so will make my family, as a whole, more:

And make my children feel_____I could also ask them what they would enjoy doing as a family, and who knows, I may learn something in the process and feel a bit like a kid again myself!

You know you're a Mother when:

- You keep up with the latest fashion, music, and trends through your 10-year-old daughter.

- You find yourself singing the tunes to Backyardigans or Hannah Montana more than songs of your genre.

- You can't even remember the simplest things because your brain cells have become mush with the birth of each child!

Step 8
Realize They Ain't Perfect But They're Yours!

Okay ladies, so I am still working on this step. Sometimes as Moms and spouses we spend a lot of our time wishing our family members were different and may try to change them. However this may cause a lot of fighting and stress that is not helpful to you or your family. Steps to acceptance of family members could include: communication, respect, seeking out the positive within each of them, trying hard not to sweat the small stuff, discussing boundaries regarding space and feelings, and realizing no one is perfect.

I've learned that, no matter how much I would like to, I cannot take a magic wand and make my husband and children be who I want them to be. Still, it would be so wonderfully exciting if I could zap them to clean up after themselves, zap them to clean up after themselves, zap them to clean up after themselves. Darn, I was hoping that if I said it three times it would work. But they are who they are. And they are mine, all mine.

My 10-year-old daughter is the slowest person (outside of me) to get dressed and ready for school in the morning. Knowing this I have tried to do different things to help her get ready, faster, in the morning so that we're both not stressed. Those things include; planning out what she is to wear for the entire week Sunday night, taking her bath at night, waking her up an half hour earlier, and turning the television on so that she will wake up to watch one of her favorite Disney shows while getting dressed.

I am also helping her to realize how blessed she is. You know the old stories our parents used to tell us about how they had to walk a mile to get to school, etc. My reaction as a child ironically was the same way as my daughters is now. I can only pray that she gets it when she's older. Instead of constantly reminding her of it (that doesn't work) I have come up with a plan on how she could give back to others who are less fortunate. Like giving things away to others that she doesn't need or finding ways she can volunteer in the church. I also try hard to spend time alone with her being she was the only child for eight years who suddenly became the big sister to three. Ultimately, I feel blessed to have a highly intelligent and responsible daughter (who was promoted a grade) that demonstrates leadership skills amongst her peers. She is also a very outgoing girl who gets along with others and is involved in several activities.

When my two year old was in the "terrible two" stage and all I could do was try, try , try to stay patient and calm when he would spread Vaseline in the VCR, throw his plate of food on the floor, or tells me to be quiet. A lot of times I did not make a fuss over things he did because I realized he was at that curious learning stage. At least that is what I try to tell myself to stay calm. However, my heart melted to hear him string together four to five word sentences when he was two. He is also one of my biggest fans when it comes to my music. He walks around the house singing songs that I wrote and I can't tell you what that does to my ego. I look forward to going through this beautiful stage with the twins as well and will just continue to pray for my sanity. However, when I look at them I realize how truly blessed I am to have them as a package deal. They are absolutely beautiful. Through out it all I love my kids unconditionally and thank God for such beautiful gifts that he has bestowed upon me.

With regards to my husband, I've had to come to terms with the fact that he can't be "my everything", my all in all, or the key to all my happiness. This is why I have other people in my life that can cater to the different parts of the complex being I am. For example, I know that my husband has a hard time listening to my endless ramblings about whatever I may be going on about at the moment. Since I know this about him, I try not to get upset and try and talk with a friend or family member who can stand to listen to my rambling moments. I can return the favor and listen to their ramblings, too.

Think back to when you first met your spouse. What drew you to him when you were dating? Was it the conversation, his personality or his dreamy eyes? Remembering back to how things were between you and your spouse could help you see the positive within each other in the present. It's highly important to communicate with your spouse on a regular basis, even if you're the only one communicating. Doing so can create a sense of intimacy, appreciation and a feeling of being heard and respected.

Realizing the strengths and differences between you and your spouse can work hand in hand if you're both willing to work together. Strength of yours could be organization, which could be the opposite for your spouse. Being so, both of you could discuss the possibility of you being the organizer in the family. Your spouse on the other hand could be strong in the area of technology, so you could utilize his skills within the household as a strength. My husband and I are different. I love to dream and converse on a regular basis, while he, on the other hand, would rather watch CNN or football. When I have an idea regarding our relationship, family or household, I like to take action and just do it. My husband has a laissez-faire attitude, and often says, "Let's think about this some more." I love to look fabulous when I go out, he could care less. It's enough to drive me mad, but then I have to realize he is who he is and remember that there are a lot more things about him that I love than things that drive me crazy. Either way, we help each other out with the strengths that we bring to the relationship. He is the go-to person for useful information and pertinent facts. He is extremely helpful, practical and responsible. I'm aware that there are plenty of things he would like to work on with me, but we'll leave that list out, because I am writing this book not him.

At a marriage retreat that my husband and I went to, they told us that married couples should try to compromise on things, meet each other halfway. It's like that old saying "If you can't beat them, join them". My husband likes to watch sports, a lot (surprise, right?) and I don't particularly. But for the sake of our relationship, rather than complain about it I could stand to watch one sports game a month with him. He could then watch one comedy or romance film with me, once a month. Doing this could bring us closer.

Another thing we learned was that the key to a successful marriage/relationship is to be selfless; to try and do things for your mate because you love them. These selfless acts promote reciprocal love and kindness. And honestly, I am taking a page out of my own book on that one as well, ladies.

What works for my husband and I is to take it one day at a time and to communicate. To get what's bothering us off our chest and move forward. Trust me when I say we have gotten into our fair share of "respectful" arguments but once we get it all out we keep it movin' without holding grudges. I say life is definitely too short. I also don't want the stress lines or the wear and tear on my body from holding onto stuff. My husband believes that we should talk about what good we have to bring into our relationship instead of focusing on what we feel is flawed. It can be easier to blame the spouse for faults and disappointments rather than the good that a person brings. What also works for us is that we allow each other to be ourselves without feeling stifled and restricted. I can be me, all of me with him. I am not afraid to tell him what's on my mind (when he's listening and awake) and he feel the same way about me. I encourage and support him when it comes to his dreams as an architect and he does the same and I've had plenty of them. In fact, I encouraged him to step out, quit his job at an architectural firm, to start his own business and he did. Now of course he had a plan and took the steps needed to do so, but he did it. He's also not judgmental and I try to be the same with him regarding situations. Yes, we have our challenges just like any other couple but again we take it one day at a time.

Setting aside time for you and your spouse is vital to your relationship and family. The time could be spent during devotion, therapy or over a cup of coffee or walking outdoors. Again, taking time out for yourselves without the kids can help rekindle the relationship and help you both focus on the positive, while strengthening your bond.

Thankfully we have God in our lives, which we can turn to when we need strength, joy, and comfort regarding our marriage and outside relationships. In addition, I have good trusting girlfriends and family members who are there for me and share similar interests as I do. Ultimately, I have learned that I have to love my family, unconditionally, for who they are. Throughout time, I had to realize that they AIN'T perfect but they're mine. I am sure my husband and kids would say the same about me.

Reflection Time - Realize They Ain't Perfect but Their Yours

Instead of complaining about my sons/daughters habit of

_____. I could try to help him/her

by_____. Something I love

about my son/daughter is_____.

He/She makes me smile when_____.

To keep my relationship with my husband strong, I could stand to compromise with him about_____or _____. Something that I am not so experienced with is_____my husband helps me with this by_____. However, I am more experienced at_____. So I help my husband out in that area. We have opposite personality characteristics when it comes to_____, but we work to complement each other's unique ways.

You know you're a Mother when:

- The last romance book you read involved a frog and a princess.

- Heaven is the sound of all your children snoring.

- The only concert you've attended within the last two years involved a singing purple dinosaur.

Section 3

Me My Fabulous Self and I

Step 9
How to be Fabulous (Or Fake It 'Til You Make It!)

You are already Fabulous by nature because of the many hats you wear, mother, wife, lover, teacher, nurturer, nurse, cook, child bearer, housekeeper, secretary, driver, playmate, life coach, etc. To juggle so many roles and keep it all together is pure fabulousness!

Fabulous can also be defined by how you feel inside and how you look on the outside. When you exude a certain level of confidence about yourself, no matter what your situation is that is fabulous.

People tend to think that once you become a mother, how you look and how you treat yourself changes and to a certain degree, that's true. The mom that used to care about her appearance has now let it all go for the sake of the kids. When you are a mom, sometimes, there is an expectation that you will look and dress a certain way that is very non-fabulous. This can be true if you let motherhood and marriage take it's toll on you. As I said earlier in the book, you have to put a little time and effort to stay on top of your looks and feelings.

So ladies, all of you own a bit of fabulousness inside. But maybe through motherhood, marriage, or complacency, you've lost sight of it.

Being fabulous can be whatever you feel it is. For me, it can also be putting on sexy heels and jeans that fit me, oh so well. Paying a couple extra dollars for those eyelashes and batting them away. Giving myself that extra Va Va Voom with a hair piece. Wearing that daring, deep red nail polish that demands attention, or a special lip gloss that makes me feel that I am ready for the world. I also love to change my hair color throughout the different seasons, depending on how I feel. In summer, I feel warm, sunny, free and bright so I like to dye my hair with streaks of gold. In the winter I usually go black or dark brown. Dying my hair black also makes me feel bold, fierce and sexy, especially with the right black outfit as a complement. These are all simple examples of how I keep it sexy but classy, not really caring what people think. Keeping up with myself makes me feel good on the inside and look good on the outside!

Now, I know there are plenty of times when you don't feel fabulous at all. Instead you feel exhausted, bloated, sick, irritable, frustrated, and the list goes on and on. Those are the times I recommend "you fake it 'til you make it". Sometimes when I look in the mirror and am irritated by what I see, I have to go into third gear and fake it. Now, faking it may mean using concealer and other makeup to cover up the bags under my eyes due to lack of sleep or to cover up the blemishes that popped up from hormonal changes. I may also opt to put on those special jeans or a favorite shirt that fits well and instantly lifts my spirits, when I look in the mirror at all that fabulousness.

Faking it may also mean putting on a smile even when you don't feel like it to help lift your spirit or someone else's. When I am going through a tough time, helping someone else by offering a listening ear, words of encouragement or an act of kindness makes me feel better as well and grateful.

Other things I have tried to do to lift my spirits and feel fabulous is to: dance or sing out loud in my house to my favorite song, drive in my car and blast a good tune, drop everything to go for a walk, or do something out of the ordinary!

Only you can be the judge of what looks and feels fabulous for you both inside and out. If you don't know, try experimenting with a new pair of shoes, jeans, nail polish or makeup that you wouldn't have used in the past. Step out of the box and try something new and exciting to feel refueled or refreshed

You don't have to spend a fortune of money on yourself to look fabulous. There are plenty of ways you can cut corners to remain fabulous on a budget.

Some of my top-notch budget beauty regimens include:

1. Getting my hair styled or getting a body massage at a really good school like the Aveda Cosmetology School. I love Aveda products. They are therapeutic and can be a little high-end but if you go to the school, you pay a fraction of the cost of going to the actual salon.
2. I don't enjoy spending all day shopping, so I go to small boutique stores to buy a few quality items that stand out and express my style without spending a fortune on my wardrobe. I have also been known to frequent outlet malls while on vacations, and thrift stores, as well. That way I can mix and match those items with what I have in my closet. It could be that bling, bling shirt, those cha cha stilettos, the "speak to me" handbag, or those ride em' girl jeans. Whatever the case may be, I always look for quality items without spending a fortune. Okay, almost always, with the exception of a good designer handbag and an occasional pair of designer shoes!
3. As I've stated earlier, I love to wear comfortable T-shirts that express what I feel, believe or think. (Another dream of mine is to design T-shirts with inspirational phrases on them regarding dreams, motherhood jokes, and fabulousness.) I also try to find pieces that accentuate my body without compromising my looks as a mother and wife at the beautiful age of thirty-something.

4. I like to get other beauty treatments done on a budget, like my eyebrow waxing, eyelash extensions, pedicures and manicures. Some of those things I could do myself if I really am sticking to a budget, like…… well, maybe none of those. I may cut corners and go to the salon to have them just paint my fingernails and toenails instead of getting the full manicure/pedicure. I also may double up at a salon that may not be so bourgeois, in other words "in the hood" to get my nails and eyelashes done at the same time, and get a discount for doing so.
5. I was told that great skin and eyebrows can make a person look years younger, so my skin is something I try hard to keep up with (at times). I don't like to spend a fortune on the latest and greatest skin regimes so; I may simply drink plenty of water, cleanse, moisturize, and exfoliate, twice a week. I like to take hot steamy showers to open up my pores and cleanse my face. Then I put a mask on. If you don't have a store-bought mask, an egg yolk makes a good mask and is wonderful for your skin. You can exfoliate and cleanse your skin with other natural products you have at home like oatmeal, cucumbers, and olive oil. Great skin, as you may know is a product of what you eat and how you take care of your body, which leads us back to Step One, taking care of yourself first- mind, body and soul!

Trying to dress sexy but classy can be a bit challenging when you constantly have baby spit up on you, but with a bit of effort you will be able to conquer the challenge of doing so. Classy can be for the day if you're working outside of the home. Sexy can be for the night, when you may be able to let your hair down and be free. I like to dress up a bit for my husband whenever we go out on a date night. He doesn't necessarily say it out loud but I know he enjoys the fact that I take out about 10.5 minutes to look fabulous for the evening. If he doesn't enjoy the way I look, trust me I do.

As stated earlier, have a few expensive pieces in your closet that you can mix and match up with a few budget friendly items. You may invest more money into something that you can wear several times throughout the month, like a good pair of shoes, handbag or a jacket. Then you can match those up with a less expensive pair of jeans, blouse or dress that compliments your shape. Inexpensive costume jewelry can also bring pizzazz to the outfit. Whatever you are wearing try going for the proper fit. Your clothes and appearance can be an expression of how you feel on the inside. How I look on the outside stems again from what I feel from within. The confidence I have comes from the time I have taken out to connect to the spirit that dwells inside of me.

Only you truly know what you need to do in order to remain fabulous on the inside, what fills you up and makes you radiate on the outside. No matter what you decide you need to do, maybe one of the best things for yourself, your husband and your children is to take out time for you. Taking time for you may ultimately help you feel better, mentally and physically, and allow you to be your best self in a sane way. If you continue to work on you, people may notice the change in you. They may see all the hard work that you put into creating a fabulous you and a fabulous family, and it will inspire them to do the same.

Now it's not always easy to get to fabulous. Just remember it is a work in progress. Be kind to yourself and look at your life to see what needs to change. It can be hard sometimes. I can relate because I lost it for a period of time. (But boy, am I glad I found it again. And fear not you will find it again, too!) After the birth of my oldest daughter, I poured a great deal of my energy into raising her, my relationship with her father, attending school and work. For years, like a lot of mothers, I pushed aside my needs for the sake of my family. I stopped doing a lot of things that made me happy like exercising, singing, hanging out with friends, and taking out time for me. I let go of myself inside and out. Often times I felt restricted to look, dress, or act a certain way because of motherhood and the relationship I was in. I didn't feel too good about myself and it showed in my spirit and my eyes. Where was my usual upbeat, optimistic self? I acted and felt quite negative towards life and others. And let me tell you, when you become a "downer", always talking about doom and gloom, people don't always want to be around you.

My relationship with God wasn't where I wanted it to be either and I believe a lot of what I went through was because of that. I didn't take out time for me or my prayer life or to listen to my inner spirit. I walked around as if a cloud was hanging over my head. During that period of time I didn't feel or act so fabulous.

I got to a point when I was really tired of feeling restless and unfilled so I began to write. I wrote about goals I wanted to complete. I wrote about how I would like my life to be and how I could change it. I wrote about other things besides my daughter that made me feel happy and fulfilled. I also begin to pray on a daily basis, building a closer relationship with God. As time went on, I began to see the results of my life changing into what I had previously written down. I was thrilled to be able to check things off in my journal that had come to pass. Little by little, I began to feel fabulous from the inside out. Shedding the layers of the sad, unfulfilled Christine into a new beautiful butterfly ready to spread her wings and fly.

If you feel you need to get back to your true self, find an outlet that will help you unleash your feelings, clear your mind and help you breathe. For me it was writing but for you it could be a craft, hobby, past time or sport. Spending time alone with your own thoughts and feelings can be very enlightening. Taking time to be with yourself can help you grow as a person. Doing so will require you to be still and get familiar with yourself again which can also take place though self reflection exercises, writing in journal and meditation. The more you learn about yourself the more empowered you will feel which will eventually lead you to spreading your fabulous wings and taking off.

Reflection Time - Ways I can be Fabulous!
The little or big things I do now that make me feel and look fabulous are:

New things that I may like to try to feel more fabulous may be:

Whatever I do, I know that I am fabulous, all the same, because I will continue to love, exercise patience and Keep It Movin'!

You know you're a Mother when:

- You've learned how to sleep like you're in a coffin because your bed is filled with children.

- You get showered and dressed at night when it's time for bed.

- You can eat breakfast, wash your face and put on your makeup in 4.5 minutes.

Step 10
Don't Stay Stuck, How to Keep it Movin'

Well ladies, this is our last step together. It sure has been fun hanging out with you for the last nine steps. I am constantly pushing myself because of the many moments where I feel overwhelmed by my busy life. I get too distracted or exhausted from the kids to focus on anything else besides getting them clean, dressed, and fed with my house somewhat intact.

Keepin' it Movin' also means recognizing that your life has different seasons. Sometimes you are on the fast track to your dreams and passions, doors are opening and opportunities are coming your way. During the summer and fall of 2009 I was performing and speaking at several venues, in the recording studio several times a month working on songs and researching this book. However in the winter and spring of 2010 my dreams were at a standstill. I was then in a different season in my life, on a slower track. I began to second-guess myself and lose focus. My dreams were taking a backseat to household projects like cleaning out the entire cluttered garage and organizing the basement. And what I realized through prayer was that it's okay to slow down. I may not have been in the studio recording my album or working on writing this book, but I was in the preparation stage for the next phase in my life. And I could completely enjoy the company of my family and revel in my clean and organized home. Your life doesn't necessarily always have to be on fast track cycle. Sometimes you have to slow down to really enjoy the details in your life which helps you appreciate what matters most. Whether your life is on the fast or slow track, try not loose sight or focus of the direction you'd like to take your life in.

It can be challenging to stay motivated and focused but if you push through and keep it Movin' you'll feel a sense of joy and satisfaction in the end.

Tips I have found helpful to Keep It Movin' include:
- Breathing
- Saying a quick one-line prayer or affirmation like-I can do all things through Christ that Strengthens me.
- Enjoy the now
- Laugh at some of the chaotic moments your kids can create, instead of crying.
- Get involved in a supportive group regarding your family, passion, or career.
- Surround yourself around positive friends or family.
- Keep an area in the house free from kid's toys and stuff.
- Try to wake up before the kids to take a few minutes for yourself and plan out the day.
- Stay one step ahead of your kids throughout the day. Example includes: preparing breakfast while kids are still sleep, preparing lunch while kids are eating breakfast, cleaning up or planning afternoon activities while kids are napping. With older kids, planning chores, or afternoon activities while at school. Have older children make their lunch the night before.
- Keep your cabinets or refrigerator stocked with easy snacks your younger kids and older can eat or grab on the go.

- Plan out summer activities for kids during the winter/spring season for the sanity of yourself and the children. Boredom can quickly set in during the summer if kids are not productively busy. I signed my three year old up for Vacation Bible School, two week summer camp, play dates, and a one day a week sports camp with his dad during the winter/spring season before classes filled up. My 12 year old was also signed up for a weekend Vacation Bible school, a volley ball camp, tennis and fashion design camp, and math/science camp ahead of time as well. They both loved the opportunity to get out and hang with friends trying out new experiences. The twins went to the day care in the gym or they went swimming, on walks, bike rides, or to the park!
- Keep lip-gloss, mascara, make-up compact or tinted moisturizer with sunscreen handy in the car!
- Have a change of shoes or clothes in the car or gym bag for you to change into for emergency purposes.
- Buy clothes that are comfortable in fabric that can be worn for bedtime and yes into the morning for gym time!
- Buy clothes that don't have to be ironed.
- Shower, shave and wash your hair at the gym or while kids are sleeping.

There have been several instances where I had to keep it Movin' or the alternative was laying down and not getting back up. One particular incident took place in summer of 2010. I had been working on my book, music, and marketing on my laptop computer where all my work had been stored. After the first of three trips it typically takes me to get all three of my kids and belongings to my truck, I discovered the driver side backseat window had been completely broken out. Glass shattered all over my babies car seats. I immediately put the twins down in my front yard and took inventory of what had been taken. The portable DVD player was missing and my laptop was also missing out of my computer bag. Instantly my heart began to race and I felt a sudden sense of sorrow. It is over, I told myself. All the work I've done over the past year and a half is gone. My dream of completing and publishing the book is to an end. Unfortunately, I had only saved the latest edition of the book on my laptop and not a flash drive. I thought I would rather the thieves take my truck than my laptop that held the key to my dreams. As I sat on the front lawn with my babies in agony, a beautiful thought floated across my mind and into my being. "Didn't your niece ask to use the laptop the night before?" I immediately ran into the house as and searched for the laptop as if my life depended on it. There it was. There was the laptop sitting in the place where my niece had left it on the arm of the couch. All I could do was immediately praise God shouting "Thank you Lord Jesus for a second chance"! All the thieves got after all was a broken portable DVD player. That experience taught me how I had no other choice but to keep it Movin'. I had lost a bit of focus in writing this book because the prior 6 months had been spent on researching agents, publishers, marketing and the technical side of writing. But it was time to get back focused on completing this book.

Sometimes you've got to improvise to keep Movin'. I know, I've got four kids! A trip to Atlanta with the whole family comes to mind. The twins were 16 months old and it was their first time on a plane. Caleb was three and Imani was 12. I was prepared for the worst so we brought my mother (who helps us out tremendously with the kids) along on the trip as well. We bought another portable DVD player for Caleb and Imani, and I packed the twins favorite books, a pack of licorice, pacifiers, sippy cups and fruit. Overall, the trip in itself went fairly well, with of course the exception of nap time and bedtime. I tried to order cribs in advance in Atlanta but was unsuccessful while staying at my sister in laws home. So we had one portable play pen and a queen size bed to split between the twins, my husband and I. We made the most out of our trip and had a great time when I was able to let go of my strict schedule with the kids and relax. I was able to visit friends and family I hadn't seen since college.

    I also auditioned for a film, attended several night events and visited museums with my family. My husband was able to visit several museums as well, which was the primary reason he wanted to go to Atlanta. He is the lead designer for the first African American museum in Minneapolis. So he drove to Alabama during our stay in Atlanta to research other African American museums along with the museums in Atlanta.

    The plane rides were quite the work though for my mother and I which was to be expected. With the exception of a few blunders, I think we did the best we could with the kids on the plane. I gave my twin girl Issa a bit too much to eat on the plane going down to Atlanta and she vomited all over me. My mother and I were exhausted from singing the itsy bitsy spider over a hundred times, playing patty cake, peek a boo and reading the same two books for over two hours. On the plane ride back, the portable DVD players' battery went out after an hour on the plane because we could not find the charger. Let's just say that's when it all went downhill with my three year old. My mother and I were sitting like mummies trying not to wake the twins after they went to sleep. However my three year old who was sitting behind us next to my peacefully sleeping husband and occupied 12 year old daughter began to get restless and shout after the DVD player went out. He was irritated, shouting out "why is my book broken!" All while slamming down the shutters on the plane. Mind you his book was actually a pamphlet to Walt Disney World that he picked up somewhere and it happened to be wrinkled. I whispered to him that I would "fix his book" when we got off the plane but that didn't work. So of course the mother who is already holding a sleeping 16 month old had to improvise again and go into third gear. I managed to switch seats with my 12 year old daughter while holding Issa the twin (who woke up) so that I could contain and entertain my three year old who was sitting next to my peacefully sleeping husband. I had to keep it Movin', for the survival and sanity of myself, my three year old and all one hundred and something passengers. I entertained the three year old and 16 month old by singing softly, giving them more treats, and taking them both one at a time on a walk to the bathroom to let them play with the water or toilet paper.

My three year old finally went to sleep after I rubbed his back, thank God. So when the plane landed, I was ever so grateful that I managed to get through the plane ride with my sanity intact. However the best part is always saved for last. My 16 month old has been known to be quite the poopy girl. Poop just always finds its way out of her pamper or bottom as soon as I let her bottom take a breather. When the plane landed and all the passengers were standing quietly to exit. My 16 month old had to poop, which was to me a good time being that we were about to get off the plane. My three year old on the other hand looks down on my seat and screams "Mommy Issa Pooped On Your Seat, Disgusting!" How mortified I was, I look down and yes there was poop occupying my seat. Again I had to improvise quickly picking up the poop with the only thing I could use in sight. Caleb's pamphlet, that he called a book. Of course he screamed "No Not My Book, There's Poop On My Book!" Soon as the aisle opened up, I quickly took him by the arm with one hand escorting him out of the plane, saying be quiet under my breath, with Issa and the poop in the other. Talk about keeping it Movin'. I left the other family members and immediately headed for the bathroom in the airport.

Other quick examples of how I managed to keep it Movin' include: Changing clothes in the car leaving a family event to a nighttime social event.
- Having only 15 minutes to do my make-up, hair and clothes before I go on to sing or speak- and still feel fabulous.

- Leaving the hair salon and deciding to kill two birds with one stone at the last minute by getting make up done at MAC and taking pictures at a one stop shop photo studio in the mall for marketing purposes.
- Keeping inexpensive, fashionable hats and sunglasses on hand for bad hair or eye days.
- Devoting at least an hour a day to work on my book, music, or exercise.
- Running out the door when my husband comes home, while the kids are literally hanging on to my legs, to pursue my dreams.
- Having the kids diaper bags pre-packed for the exodus trip from the house to the car.
- Pre-packing the kids' lunch to eat in the car on their food trays, after a morning at the gym or the library, on the drive home.
- Having diapers, wipes, snacks, portable DVD player, extra clothes, children songs CDs, and traveling cloth seat covers stored in the car.
- Bathing the kids the night before and Yes! Getting them dressed for the next day.

Keep it Movin' is an attitude that is manifested through your actions. As a mom, having a "keep it Movin'" attitude can help you to push through and enjoy life regardless of what may be thrown at you. If I can do it with four small kids so can you! Most importantly it will allow you to be free. Even just for a moment to breathe and let go, to dream, to celebrate and remain true to you.

I pray that you step out and continue to be the fabulous woman that you already are! When things feel tough, keep in mind that this is a season a small short time in your life, so push yourself to get up, get through and Keep it Movin'!

Appendix

Appendix A
Steps to Put Together Portfolio Christine's Plan

I will leave you with personal resources I created for myself to turn my dreams into a reality. Materials consist of drafts including my portfolio I used for marketing purposes, a time line, a budget list, songs lyrics I wrote which will be featured on my CD, "Christine FREE: The Evolution of DREAMZ", and a book proposal I submitted to literary agencies seeking representation. However, in the end after several years of research I decided to publish myself through my own publishing company Belfrey Books.

Book:
- Write draft manuscript
- Send manuscript to editor
- Make Changes to manuscript
- Publishing Company Choices
- Send manuscript to agents and traditional publishers
- Research self-publishing companies

Music:
- Get the recorded version of Illusion and A Lil' Longer
- Contact Musicians for Beautiful Butterfly and Fabulous and FREE

- Fabulous & Free - Trumpet Player, Salsa feel, Uptempo
- Beautiful Butterfly - Strings, ocean feel, breeze
- Illusion-Bass player, Drummer-Funky feel-Gritty - strong beats
- Compose Music
- Network with producers
- Research Business side of music industry, digital-contracts, rights, legality, writing lyrics for others, etc.
- Record Beautiful Butterfly, Fabulous & FREE and Illusion with new music

Time line

Send Book proposal out to 6 Agents between April 5th and April 9th, it takes 3 months to hear back April, May, June.
- If I do not hear anything back by 4th week of May I will Self Publish
- Website/T-shirts/SINGLE Come out in May around Mother's Day.

6 months April - Sept. to:
- Network/Build up marketability thru
    1. Facebook
    2. My Website
    3. My business
    4. Lisa-Publicist
    5. Search for a Manager
    6. Twitter
    7. Twittermom
    8. Blogging
    9. LinkedIn
- Sing my songs around town to get my name out!
- Write 5 new songs
- Build my website
- Work on business cards

- Possibilities for my office;
- Part time Life Coach
    - Meets with clients to help guide them on their journey to discovering their dreams and goals.
    - Uses my journal template

Website Blog: **Girlfriends Corner**-Blogging Subjects could be:
- How to reach dreams
- Advice on college
- Marriage/Communication
- Problem solving
- Children
- Education
- Spirituality
- Relationships

December, January, February, March to work on songs-for future CD –Totaling 12 songs.

Budget
Photography:
- Makeup
- Outfit
- Hair
- T-shirts Line

Music:
- Musicians/Recording
- Studio room for musicians
- CDs

Book:
- Editor 1st draft
- Draft proposal
- Manuscript 2nd draft
- Self-publish route

Marketing/Promotion
- Website
- Business Cards
- Marketing cost

Appendix B
Song Lyrics by Christine Free

Illusion

Verse 1:

>Something that appears to be,
>Is not what it seems to be
>Will it break you or will it make you?
>Who can help you with reality?
>The girl in me didn't wanna see
>The girl in me didn't wanna know
>All the hurt, the pain and all the misery
>The god in me is trying to set me free!

Chorus:

>Do you wanna know, would you wanna know
>Can you handle it, or will you shatter it
>Do you wanna know, really wanna know
>Illusion, Illusion

Chorus:

> Do you wanna know, would you wanna know
> Can you handle it, or will you Shatter it
> Do you wanna know, really wanna know
> Illusion, Illusion

Verse 2:

> And what about the community?
> We only see what we wanna see
> That inner child, that broken man
> Armed with guns at yo command!

Bridge:

> The Hurting girl
> Background Vocal
> Do you see?
> The Hurting girl
>
> Can you hear?
> The Hurting girl
> Do you know?

Bridge:

> The Hurting girl
> Background Vocal
> Do you see?
> The Hurting girl
>
> Can you hear?
> The Hurting girl
> Do you know?

She keeps her secrets on the inside
At the expense of his hand

She's really dying on the inside
Does she know God has the healing plan!

Chorus:

> Do you wanna know, would you wanna know
> Can you handle it, or will you shatter it
> Do you wanna know, really wanna know
> Illusion, Illusion

Verse 3:

Unveil her beauty and you will see
All the pain, the shame and insecurities

You'd think she's happy forever more
Who can help her unlock the door?

He has the game he numbs the pain
From the abuse - that makes him - wanna go insane

Someone reach out to that little boy
Who can help him really understand?
Someone reach out to that inner child

Someone help him be a better man!
Open our eyes

Background Vocal:

> Solution
> Open our ears
> Solution
> Open our hearts
> Solution
> So we can give
> Open our eyes
> Solution
> Open our ears
> Solution
> Open our hearts
> Solution
> So we can give!

A Lil Longer

Verse 1:

> One night I was home alone
> Feeling low
> Feeling all alone
> Then I heard his voice calling me
> He said
> Please don't, please don't
> Give up on me.
>
> One day I was driving home
> Feeling all hope was gone.
> Then I heard his voice telling me
> He said he'll be
> Be there to comfort me.

Chorus:

Just Hold On

Background Vocal:

He whispered in my ear
Hold On

You're time to shine is near.
A Lil Longer
A Lil Longer
Hold On
Believe His Word is True
Hold On
He'll work it out for you.
A Lil Longer
A Lil Longer

Verse 2:

Broken, I was sad and down
No one to turn to
Going down.
Then I heard his voice calling me
He said
Please don't, please don't
Give up on me.

Stronger now
I am full of joy
All things are possible
I dream of more.
Cause I know his love blesses me
And he's there.
Right there to carry me

Chorus:

Just Hold On

Background Vocal:

He whispered in my ear
Hold On

You're time to shine is near.
A Lil Longer
A Lil Longer
Hold On
Believe His Word is True
Hold On
He'll work it out for you.
A Lil Longer
A Lil Longer

Bridge:

Hold onto your Dreams girl
Never let your Dreams Die
Have Faith and Trust and Believe in Him
Hold fast, be Strong Chile' and you Shall Win

Believe his Word is True
He'll Work it out For You, Now!
Just Have Faith, and Trust and Believe in Him
Hold fast, Be Strong Chile' and you Shall Win

And Hold on
Be Strong
A Lil Longer
A Lil Longer

Beautiful Butterfly

Verse 1:

> I woke up this morning, I dreamed of transforming
> A doctor, a lawyer, writer, performer.
> I know he will guide me, if I just believe him
>
> I just wanna be Free
> To feel the wind beneath me
> For I've been restored to
> To go on this journey

> Chorus:
>
>> Beautiful Butterfly, believes she can Reach the sky.
>> Beautiful Butterfly, Oh Beautiful Butterfly
>> Beautiful Butterfly, believes she can Touch the sky
>> Beautiful Butterfly, Oh beautiful butterfly

Verse 2:

> Your dreams will come true, if you just believe him
> God will not leave you
> He will
> He'll come thru
> He will restore me.
> If I just receive him
>
> I just wanna be Free
> To feel the wind beneath me
> For I've been restored to
> To go on this journey

Chorus:

>Beautiful Butterfly,
>Believes she can Reach the sky.
>Beautiful Butterfly,
>Oh Beautiful Butterfly
>Beautiful Butterfly,
>Believes she can Touch the sky
>Beautiful Butterfly,
>Oh Beautiful Butterfly

Bridge:

>Spreads your wings and Fly
>Spreads your wings and Fly away
>Dare to dream and Fly
>Dare to dream you'll be okay,

>Spreads your wings and Fly
>Spreads your wings and Fly away
>Dare to dream and Fly
>Dare to dream you'll be okay,

Chorus:

>Beautiful Butterfly,
>Believes she can Reach the sky.
>Beautiful Butterfly,
>Oh Beautiful Butterfly
>Beautiful Butterfly,
>Believes she can Touch the sky
>Beautiful Butterfly,
>Oh Beautiful Butterfly

Beautiful Butterfly

Fabulous and Free

Verse 1:

> I know, I been, so sad I've been down and
> Broken, torn and, So low nowhere to go
> Been there, done that, so tired of hurtin
> Crying, tryin, no hope for tomorrow
>
> Doubters, haters, oh no she can't make it
> She stuck in, a box and
> She can't get up out it.
>
> You didn't know, I had him.
> On my side and with him,
> I will, survive cause,
> She can't live without him
> He blessed me, renewed me,
> Now that I am Free, I
> Know that, with him I
> Will make it to the top, Oh!

Chorus:

> Fabulous and Free,
> I feel I am Fabulous and Free
>
> I am just gone be me,
> I know I am Fabulous and Free
> No need to agree,
> Believe I am Fabulous and Free
> Oh, Can't you see,
> That I am Fabulous and Free

Verse 2:

> Tried to,
> Please you,
> But I had to let go
> Had to,
> Surrender,
> To the voice and be Free
> Wiser,
> Stronger,
> The sun is shining brighter
> So free to,
> Be me and,
> Be the best I can
>
> You didn't know,
> I had him.
> On my side and with him,
> I will,
> Survive cause,
> I can't live without him
> He blessed me,
> Renewed me,
> Now that I am Free I
> Know that,
> With him I,
> Will make it to the top, Oh!

Chorus:

    Fabulous and Free,
    I feel I am Fabulous and Free

    I am just gone be me,
    I know I am Fabulous and Free
    No need to agree,
    Believe I am Fabulous and Free
    Oh, Can't you see,
    That I am Fabulous and Free

Bridge:
    I choose, I choose, I choose, I choose, I choose
    I choose to be me!
    I choose to be free!

    I choose, I choose, I choose, I choose, I choose
    I choose the light!
    I choose to have joy!

    I choose, I choose, I choose, I choose, I choose
    I choose to be free!
    Be the best I can be!

Chorus:

    Fabulous and Free,
    I feel I am Fabulous and Free
    I am just gone be me,
    I know I am Fabulous and Free
    No need to agree,
    Believe I am Fabulous and Free
    Oh, Can't you see,
    That I am Fabulous and Free

Appendix C
Sample Letters and Proposal Christine's Proposal

Query letter:
January 29th, 2010

Jane Smith
President
New York, NY

Dear Ms. Smith:

I am submitting *"Ladies Keep it Movin'… 10 Steps for Staying Sane and Fabulous with Kids, Your Man and a DREAM!"*

In order to stay sane and healthy as a mother, lover or wife, there are times when putting yourself first is a must. Okay ladies, that doesn't mean going out and buying yourself that Coach bag before buying groceries for the household (whoops, I may have done that!) or hanging all day with the ladies sipping Mai Tai's on the beach before taking care of your children and checking in with your man (what a nice fantasy, though).

This self-help book is the synthesis of my life's journey from a young unwed mother putting herself through college to a teacher with a master's in education, who is now married with four children. Publishing *Ladies Keep it Movin'* is the culmination of my dream to reinvent myself as an author; singer and speaker who will one day soon appear on the Oprah Winfrey show.

    The reader also receives something more, a CD single of a song I wrote and recorded, called "A lil Longer."
    To see the manuscript please check "YES", below and return this letter in the enclosed reply envelope.

Sincerely,

Christine FREE

( ) YES I'd like to see Ladies Keep it Movin'
( ) No, but thanks for asking.
( ) Please query_____at the agency and say Jane Smith sent you.
Enclosure: SASE

Inquiry Letter:
January 29th, 2010

Jane Smith
President

New York, NY

Dear Ms. Smith:

I am submitting my manuscript, *"Ladies Keep it Movin'… 10 Steps for Staying Sane and Fabulous with Kids, Your Man and a DREAM!"*

Ladies Keep it Movin' is a self-help book geared towards women and mothers who are interested in actively pursuing their dreams despite the roles they are often required to play in their families and in society. The book lays out my tried and true 10-step process for feeling fabulous inside and out and making my dreams a reality while juggling four kids and a husband. Besides the ten, easy to follow steps, the book includes quirky mothering quotes, inexpensive beauty tips and self-reflection exercises.

My book has down home advice from a middle class mom, who follows her dreams no matter what life throws at her, including infant twins! The reader also receives, a CD single of a song I wrote and recorded, called "A lil Longer", (from the soon to be released album "Christine FREE The Evolution of DREAMZ"). I believe Belfrey Books can make my dream a reality.

I have included the following: Introduction, Outline, Text Sample Chapters, Biography, Market Analysis, Photographs, and Song.

If you have any questions please contact me by telephone at 555-555-5555 and through email at info@christinefree.com.

Thank you for your consideration,

Christine FREE

Introduction to the Book
As a mother of four children, who recently gave birth to a set of twins, I am constantly being approached by people who want to know my secret. How do I, a middle class mother, find the time and energy to be fabulous while pursuing my dreams? How do I juggle it all and still look and feel great? In the process of telling so many people how I managed to be a mom, a wife and still go after my dream, I realized that I had a pretty amazing system in place. And it was working! So, I wrote this book to let women know what I know about having a whirlwind, yet fulfilling life.

It's no secret that a mother's needs and dreams tend to get pushed aside when taking care of the needs of others. While there are various books on balancing motherhood, raising children, and hanging on to a healthy sense of self," Ladies Keep it Movin", 10 Steps for Staying Sane and Fabulous with Kids, Your Man and a Dream" is one of the first books to focus on a mother's need for being fabulous while taking steps to pursue huge dreams along with raising wonderful children and keeping her man happy. Being fabulous inside and out comes from a "just do it" attitude, taking the necessary steps to be happy, loving yourself first, and then taking care of your mind, soul and body.

The ten easy to follow steps in this book are divided into three sections. Section One explains how to discover the different parts of yourself, mind, body and soul and take good care of them. In Section One, I also unveil how I rediscovered my dreams as a mother and how you can too. I explain specific actions I took towards making my dreams a reality as a singer and writer. Section Two speaks to the need for support from outside resources so you can raise your family and do all you have to do to be who you are and go for what you want. This section also stresses the importance of family time and gives you some creative ideas. Section Three deals with the innate fabulousness of all mothers and how to embrace it and bring it to the forefront of who you are. Here I share some inexpensive beauty and fashion tips as well.

So read on to find out how I've maintained sanity in the pursuit of my dreams while taking care of a family of six.

Section I - How to Stay Sane Nurturing the Inner Me, Woman, Mother, Wife, Lover

<u>Step 1 - Take Care of Yourself First - Mind, Body, and Spirit</u>
This step focuses on the different parts of self and how to nurture mind, body, and spirit so you can be fabulous and take care of your family in a sanely manner. There are lots of inexpensive ways to nourish yourself that incorporate family time like having sex with the hubby or going on family walks for exercise. Also, reading something uplifting or taking time to pray feeds the mind and the soul. The ultimate way I've been able to remain sane and fabulous is by nourishing my spiritual life. Taking care of yourself is the foundation of all the other steps.

<u>Step 2 - Be True to Who You Are Aside from Being a Mom and a Wife</u>
Being true to who you are gives you a strength that radiates out from the core of your existence and dictates your destiny. I share the journey I've taken to uncover my true self. Being passionate, complex, artistic, sexy and free to be yourself can happen no matter what titles you carry around as wives, mothers, and women. You'll be inspired to discover your own identity with self-reflection exercises.

<u>Step 3 - Dare to Dream! And Find Your Passion</u>
Dreams and passion are vital to feeling fabulous. Step Three encourages you to unearth your passion and go for your dreams no matter what lies in your daily path. Here I lay out the necessary actions to realize your dreams. For inspiration, I talk specifically about my own dreams, which include being the first in my immediate and extended family to graduate

from college and receive three degrees by my target age of thirty, reinventing myself from a teacher to an author, singer and speaker who will one day appear on the Oprah Winfrey Show. This step will give you a sense of purpose in pursuing your own dreams.

Step 4 - Slow Down, Breathe and Relax!
This step focuses on how to deal with the many moments of chaos and absentmindedness a mom deals with from birthing to raising children. I'll show you how to refuel so you don't go to extremes like running away to take an unaffordable vacation, shopping until you drop (both of which I've tried myself and believe me they don't work in the long run!) Stress really takes a toll on your fabulousness. I also make some useful suggestions for slowing down, breathing and relaxing.

Section II - How to Stay Sane When Balancing Family, Kids, Husband, and Work

Step 5 - Get Organized - Calendars and Routines Are a Necessity
Getting organized is all about the importance of providing structure and routines for the family. Life just flows better when everyone in your house knows what to do or what to expect on a daily and weekly basis. Putting family game nights, school happenings, special occasions, and sporting events, in your Blackberry, Icalendar or a good old fashioned planner (my calendar of choice!) assists a fabulous mom in keeping track of her busy world. Your relationship will fare better too, with scheduled date nights, sex nights, or some planned down time to discuss your family's future. It is extremely important that I adhere to a daily schedule while raising infant twins, a two year old and a pre teen for their sense of well being as well as mine! Letting your life run wild will lead to moments of insanity.

Step 6 - Don't Be Afraid to Ask or Pay for Help - You Can't Do It All! It Takes a Village

Be honest with yourself. When you realize that you can't do it all alone then you can get serious about rounding up some much needed help. Learning to delegate chores I've been told is a gift I posses and love to pass on. I won't hesitate to ask the kid next door or a relative dropping by for a helping hand. Whether you get support from friends and family or pay for help, your sanity and fabulousness depends on your ability to reach out. This step offers up some creative resources and teaches you ways to get assistance with managing your children and your home life. Enlisting support from others frees you up to enjoy your life and family in your own way.

Step 7 - Make Time for Family, Yeah!

A fabulous family needs time to be with each other and to have some fun. Scheduled and unscheduled time together allows your family to enjoy each other's company and strengthens the family bond. This step includes lots of "family time" suggestions and tips for combining work, play and exercise in making your family a priority.

Step 8 - Realize They Ain't Perfect, But They're Yours!

Imperfections and differences in yourself and your family members can really get in the way of a harmonious existence. Step eight helps you learn to let go, compromise, or move forward. I talk about the lessons that I learned so I could love myself and my family unconditionally. Things like defining marriage for myself and creating space for my children's feelings without judging them. Believing you can change your husband or certain habits of your child, again only leads to moments of insanity. Letting go of expectations is love and invaluable for the family.

Section III - Me, My Fabulous Self and I

<u>Step 9 - How to be Fabulous (or fake it 'til you make it!)</u>
Fabulous is defined by how you feel inside and how you look on the outside. And mothers are just plain fabulous by nature because of the many roles you have to juggle as lovers, teachers, cooks, playmates and nurses. Here, I explain the process I undertook in learning that I can be sexy, a Christian, believe in myself and still be a good mom. I've gone through periods of dark times because I was unhappy being someone I wasn't, wishing I possessed a talent someone else had. However, after much soul searching and praying, I've come to love the person I am and the gifts I have. This section encourages us mothers to bring out the fabulous side of ourselves regardless of all the expectations society, husbands and kids may place on us. Dancing or singing out loud to your favorite tune, experimenting with a new style, or stepping out of the box to try something new to refuel and rekindle that fabulous side.

<u>Step 10 - Don't Stay Stuck. How to Keep it Movin'</u>
Last but not least this step explains how I've been able to look or feel fabulous without breaking the bank and how you can, too. Finding creative ways to receive quality services or clothing items is essential for me as a fabulous mother of four on a budget. Whether it's wearing those "ride 'em" girl jeans that make you feel so hot or mixing up a designer handbag with a secondhand store shirt in just the right color. Some of my inexpensive beauty regimens include receiving services at a fabulous cosmetology school for my hair and body. I offer websites and resources for moms to have at their fingertips that will assist them towards feeling and looking fabulous.

Text Sample Chapters
Step 1, Step 2, Step 3-Partial Chapter

(Chapters not inserted here again for the reader)

Market Analysis

This book will appeal to mothers, wives, stay at home mothers, women interested in having children, and working mothers seeking a change and are interested in pursuing their dreams. There are 154.7 million females in the United States as of Oct. 1, 2008.

The estimated number of mothers of all ages in the United States is 82.8 million according to data from the Survey of Income and Program Participation. 62.6 million was the number of married women (including those who were separated or had an absent spouse) in 2007. Lastly, 5.6 million is the number of stay-at-home mothers nationwide in 2007, up from 4.6 million a decade earlier according to the Families and Living Arrangements: 2007 Census.

Readers will be interested in "Ladies Keep it Movin' 10 Steps for Staying Sane and Fabulous with Kids, Your Man and a DREAM" because of the quirky title that speaks to how one can juggle the many things in life yet still be able to pursue their passion in a fabulous fashion. Mothers tend to loose themselves in their children, husband and house. This book will inspire mothers to find or pursue their dreams and livelihood.

Ladies Keep It Movin' speaks to the trends of: parenting, motherhood, mind, body and spirit, self-help and personal development.

I will use the mass media arts and teaching degree I've obtained to market the book by public speaking in television shows, radio shows, conferences, workshops, book clubs, church groups, mommy groups, etc. In addition, I will utilize my teaching degree and background to create a goal dream journal to accompany the book. My performance and singing background will also work for me to promote this book within the music industry.

Book 1 offers tools to use when dealing with the many stressful facets of parenting but Ladies Keep It Movin' has a

Christian message that is a selling point. My spiritual life is ultimately what keeps me sane and fabulous. My book also gives the reader simple, enlightening, humorous and straight forward, methods I've used to deal with the chaos of family life that the average mother can relate to and identify with. Ladies Keep It Movin' is also written for the busy on the go mom with a limited amount of time and a short attention span (like me).

Book 2 is broken into three sections similar to my book which is taking care of self, balancing the many hats of motherhood, and dealing with the family. However Ladies Keep it Movin' also has motherhood jokes and reflection pages at the end of each chapter. You know you're a mother when: making love to your husband takes place now, while you're napping and you wake up and ask, "Are you done yet?" The quirky jokes after each chapter allows the mother to find humor in parenting, connecting with another mother through similar experiences. Additionally, the reflection pages, personalizes what was read after each chapter allowing the reader to implement practices into her own life.

Book 3 focuses on what it means to be a mom and offers tools to guide the mom in nurturing herself. What stands out in my book is that I not only offer suggestions and tools to assist the mom in unveiling her true self but I also walk the reader through steps I've taken in the pursuit of my dreams. Sharing my journey allows the reader to connect with my experiences and offers them strategies to use for turning their dreams into a reality as well. The reader will receive a CD of a song I wrote and recorded allowing them to be a part of a dream come true for a middle income mom of four. In addition, I encourage the reader to step away from expectations society, family or friends places on us daring us to be whoever we want to be.

Book 4 frequently refers to certain words like sexy throughout the book referring to a certain lifestyle relating to multitasking and motherhood. Doing so can be a bit confusing according to the accurate definition of the word. Ladies Keep It Movin', offers clear cut steps giving the reader what they want based on the title and chapters. Being fabulous can be defined by how you look or feel and my book offers realistic examples relating to: exercise, spirituality, fashion, organization, relationships, and dreams.

Book 5 shares similarities for offering advice and suggestions that are interwoven with personal stories of our lives. However, I also give the reader insights on how I've maintained sanity in an non traditional way by "letting go" of the notion of perfection within my household and family. In the chapter, Realize They Ain't Perfect But They're Yours, I give the reader tips on being a mom in the 21st century like: running out the door on a Saturday morning before any one wakes up, Or coming to an agreement with your husband-or yourself (if you're the only one who agrees) with time you need to set aside during the week for yourself for work or play. Sometimes mothers have to push down emotional ties, believing that we have to do it all and think like the hubby at times to feel refueled.

www.ingramcontent.com/pod-product-compliance
Lightning Source LLC
LaVergne TN
LVHW011209080426
835508LV00007B/684